GETTING TO
"CLOSED"

Also by Stephan Schiffman

Cold Calling Techniques (That Really Work!)

Sales Don't Just Happen

Make It Happen Before Lunch

High Efficiency Selling

The Consultant's Handbook

The 25 Sales Habits of Highly Successful Salespeople

GETTING TO
"CLOSED"

STEPHAN SCHIFFMAN

Dearborn™
Trade Publishing
A **Kaplan Professional** Company

Vice President and Publisher: Cynthia A. Zigmund
Editorial Director: Donald J. Hull
Acquisitions Editor: Mary B. Good
Senior Project Editor: Trey Thoelcke
Interior Design: Lucy Jenkins
Cover Design: Richard Bresden
Typesetting: Elizabeth Pitts

Library of Congress Cataloging-in-Publication Data

Schiffman, Stephan.
   Getting to "closed" : a proven program to accelerate the sales cycle and increase commissions / Stephan Schiffman.
      p.   cm.
Includes index.
   ISBN 0-7931-5389-1
   1. Selling. 2. Sales management.   I. Title.
   HF5438.25 .S3342   2002
   658.8'1—dc21

                                                        2002003512

DEDICATION

To Jennifer and Daniele

Contents

Acknowledgments   ix
Introduction: How This System Came About   xi

PART ONE
The Fundamentals

1. What You're Holding in Your Hands Increases Sales   3
2. 15, 7, and 1 (And Other Useful Insights on the Sales Process)   7
3. Mastering the Sales Process   19
4. Common Questions about the Sales Process   33
5. Monitoring Your Numbers   39

PART TWO
Learning the System

6. Don't Wait for No   45
7. The Opportunity Column   53
8. The Closed Column   59
9. The First Appointment Column   63
10. The 50 Percent Column   69
11. The 90 Percent Column   77
12. The 25 Percent Column   81

13. Reinforcing the Categories   85
14. Tracking Changes in Your Board over Time   93
15. Common Questions about the Prospect Management System   101

PART THREE

Getting Up and Running

16. The Art of the Board Review   107
17. Using Team Selling to Rescue Lost Sales   113
18. Forecasting   117
19. Case Study: Increasing Revenue with the Prospect
    Management System   121
20. Ten Principles for Sales Success   125

    Answers to Chapter Quizzes   127
    Appendix A: Your Monday Morning Sales Meeting   129
    Appendix B: Board Ranking/Questions Tool   141
    Appendix C: Contact Categorization Exercise   143
    Appendix D: Sales Scenarios   155
    Appendix E: The Prospect Board and Time Management   169
    Index   177

Acknowledgments

This book would not have been possible without the help and assistance of a number of individuals. I want to begin by acknowledging the help and encouragement of the good people at Dearborn, including Mary Good, a tireless advocate for this project who "got it" the minute we first outlined the idea; Leslie Banks, who has helped so much with marketing and promotion; and Trey Thoelcke, whose patience knew no bounds.

Thanks also go out to the team members at D.E.I. Management Group who contributed in so many ways, large and small, to the evolution of this project: Brandon Toropov, who helped this material make the critical transition from in-person training to published book; Lynne Einleger; Steve Bookbinder; Stacia Skinner; Raul Nunez; Gino Sette; Tina Bradshaw; Michele Reisner; Nancy Bellard; Martha Rios; Anganie Ali; Lesha Connell; David Rivera; Scott Forman; Fredrik Rydlun; Alan Koval; and Surendra Sewsankar.

My gratitude also goes out to Stephanie Kip Rostan and Daniel Greenberg at James Levine Communications, and to John

Sadler of Sadler Recording, who helped us to assemble the recorded materials that support this book.

Special thanks, of course, are due to Jennifer, Daniele, and Anne for offering, as always, their love and support.

Introduction
How This System Came About

How did I learn about the phases customers go through before they turn into commissions? What launched this system for identifying, organizing, and managing prospects?

Many years ago, I took what has to be a fateful step in the life of any entrepreneur: I hired my first salesperson, a bright and capable guy I'll call Doug.

For six months, Doug and I worked hard. We called lots of people. We met with lots of people. But we didn't really manage our activity effectively, and we had no good estimate of how that activity would actually translate, over time, into revenue for us.

Ours was a hit-and-miss operation and, to be frank, we spent much more time than I would have liked on the misses.

I was frustrated at my inability to get to the bottom of what Doug's work—and, yes, my work—was really adding up to. One Friday afternoon as we were wrapping up for the day, I had an idea. I suggested to Doug that he and I spend the following morning in the office together talking about prospects so we could get a better feeling for exactly what the future held for us.

Doug agreed, and he came in with a stack of blue index cards. Each of the cards bore the name of one of his prospect companies.

With Doug seated across from me, I took the first card, read off the company name—let's say it was the Acme Company—and said, "Okay, Doug, how do you think we should rank this?"

He said, "Rank it?" His uncertain glance made it clear that he wanted me to explain exactly what I was suggesting. I wasn't entirely sure what I was getting at, but I decided to press on; something inside me seemed to understand, at least at an intuitive level, what I'd just asked Doug to do.

"Yeah," I continued, "how would you rank it?"

"What do you mean?" he asked.

"Is it ready to close? Are we starting from scratch? Is it somewhere in between? What are we looking at?"

Doug looked at the ceiling. He now understood what I was asking. I now understood what I was asking. I watched him as he thought for a long moment.

"I guess I'd say it's about 50-50," he finally said.

"Okay," I continued. "Then let's put it right here in the middle. We'll use the Acme Company as a kind of baseline. This is our 50-50 point." I placed the first card in the middle of my desk.

I picked up the next card—let's say it was the Brockton Corporation. "How about this one?" I asked.

"What about it?" said Doug.

"Well, if Acme is our baseline, and Acme represents a prospect that's 50-50, one that could go either way, does Brockton go above it, below it, or in the exact same spot?"

Doug thought for a moment, then he did something absolutely essential: He used a specific set of sales criteria to classify a specific group of prospects.

"Steve," he said, "the more I think about it, the more I have to say that I think I made a mistake a minute ago with Acme. I think Brockton should be our 50-50 baseline, and I'll tell you why. I've actually been to Brockton three or four of times, and I've only met with Acme twice. I think I understand Brockton's business, what they're trying to do and how they do it. I've submitted a proposal, and now I'm just waiting to hear what happens next. So because of all that, I'd have to say that Brockton is the real 50-

50 card. At Acme, I've had a good meeting, but I haven't had a chance to develop a proposal yet."

I said, "Fine. Then we'll call that one 50-50." And with that, we were no longer going on hunches or gut instincts. We had a clear set of criteria for the prospects we felt had a 50 percent chance of closing.

We moved on to the next card. "What can you tell me about Crystal Industries?" I asked.

"That one's golden," he said. "Crystal is absolutely the best prospect I have."

When I pressed Doug to explain what made Crystal significantly better than Brockton, he explained that the president of Crystal had given him a verbal agreement to do business with us. I asked him whether he would be willing to bet $100 that the sale would go through. He said he was and that sounded good to me, so I placed the card for Crystal to the right of the one for Brockton. Suddenly we had another criterion: the verbal agreement.

At that point we had three cards on my desk: one at 50 percent, one that looked to have a better than one-in-two chance to close, and one that seemed somewhat less likely than that to close.

I pulled the next card from Doug's pile and asked, "Okay, what's the story with Doubleplex Industries?"

Doug sighed. "Doubleplex. That guy's driving me nuts. I've been calling and calling, and he just doesn't respond. He never calls me back."

I put the card all the way over to the left—off the charts, as it were—and said, "Don't worry about it." I didn't know it, but I was creating a brand new category: the fallback category, for people we had spoken to once, but who had fallen back to inactive status.

The next card was Everclear, Incorporated. I said, "What can you tell me about them?"

"Everclear. Gee, I haven't even called them yet."

I placed that card with Doubleplex. This was an opportunity for future selling. I grouped it together with the card that had fallen back.

Next was Fairway Corporation. "What's happening here?" I asked.

Doug told me he had scheduled a first appointment with the president of this company, but hadn't actually gone on the visit yet. This seemed like an entirely different animal than the companies we'd talked about thus far. It was definitely to the left of the 50 percent baseline, but it wasn't exactly an opportunity or a fallback.

I decided to place this card to the right of the pile I'd placed the he-won't-call-back and I-haven't-called-them-yet cards in, but *before* the group of people we'd already met with at least once. This group, in other words, was for people we had scheduled meetings with, but hadn't met yet. I didn't know it at the time, but this group was eventually to emerge as the most important of them all. (You'll learn why a little later in this book.)

If you're a little perplexed about all the different categories, don't worry. The later chapters of this book will clear everything up. For now, just bear in mind that we worked for a couple of hours, added a group for businesses with which we already had formal written commitments, and ended up with six groups of cards spread out on my desk (as shown at the right).

Notice that the likelihood of closing the sale *increases* as you move from left to right in the above diagram. On the far right-hand side, we have people who've actually signed contracts: that's 100 percent. On the far left-hand side, we have people who have made *no* commitment to us, but with whom we want to do business someday: that's zero percent likelihood. The other groups increase in likelihood as they get closer to the right-hand side.

As I say, by the end of the day, we had taken all 30 of our active prospects and sorted them out. They were spread out all over my desk, in the categories I've just described to you.

Once we had everything categorized, I had an idea.

I put each of the groups up on a bulletin board on my wall. I had to take a lot of other things off the board to make room, but I managed. As I transferred the cards, I reinforced what we had decided in terms of criteria for each of the people in the group.

People who haven't called us back and people we want to call but haven't called yet	People who have agreed to meet with us for the first time	People we've met with at least once, but who aren't yet at the 50% baseline	50% baseline: People who have a proposal that makes sense and are seriously thinking about working with us	People who have given us a verbal agreement to do business	Closed: contract finalized

LIKELIHOOD OF CLOSING DEAL →

0%   *100%*

"These people are closed. These people have given us a verbal agreement to do business. These people are 50-50." And so on.

Once we had everything up on the board, I realized that we had a new way of looking at our business. Suddenly, at a glance, we knew exactly what we had. We could tell how many first appointments we had scheduled, and we could tell how that total compared to the number of prospects we had in our 50-50 group. (What we *didn't* yet realize was the role that time and our own company's sales cycle would play in evaluating those groups as prospects graduated from one group to the next or fell off the active part of the board. You'll be learning a lot about time cycles in the main chapters of this book.)

Once we posted the prospects in their various categories on the bulletin board, stepped back, and evaluated what we saw, we had an instant snapshot of our prospect base. We knew exactly where we stood, and we knew what categories needed to be improved. What's more, when we talked through the cards on the board, we both *agreed* on what we ought to do to advance each of the prospects under discussion. This was pretty remarkable because Doug and I had spent a fair amount of time up to that point adding up groups and arguing over our respective gut feelings about what individual companies were likely to do. Now, with just a few simple criteria, a stack of index cards, some tacks, and a bulletin board, we had a much better picture of what was going on.

Suddenly, we were strategizing forward movement within the individual accounts instead of arguing over whether or not they would close. For instance, we now had a clear goal for the companies immediately to the left of our 50-50 group. We wanted to get these companies *into* that 50-50 category, and to do that, we had to try to schedule another meeting so we could get the information we needed in order to put together a good proposal.

At the end of the meeting, I said to Doug, "You know what? This is great. Let's leave these cards up on the board and update them as things change." Doug wasn't crazy about this idea—maybe because he realized that that meant I would know *exactly* what was going on in his prospect base at all times. I insisted, though, and that bulletin board stayed on that wall for five years. (It only came down because we wore it out and had to replace it with a new magnetic board that I designed.)

When the cards went up on that bulletin board, our entire selling philosophy changed. We became focused on how to move prospects forward. The board gave us a reason to ask, "How, specifically, can we move this prospect from where it is now to the next category over?"

In fact, that afternoon I changed the way I ran my business. Regular meetings to review and update the board became something of an obsession for me. I've been running my company "by the board" ever since.

That's how the system in this book came into existence. What's really interesting is that I never intended to use the categories we developed as a training program! I simply thought of them as internal tools that helped us manage our own business effectively and increase sales. They certainly did that! Then came the day when I was talking to a client of ours who had taken every sales training program we had to offer. My contact asked me, "Steve, what else have you got? What's next for us?"

Almost without thinking, I started outlining the "next program in our sequence": the Getting to Closed (or Prospect Management) program. Although I had never used this as-yet-nonexistent training program, I was certainly familiar with the system!

I talked the client through the categories, explained what they meant, and demonstrated how they could help her people build up their base of business, predict income effectively, and maintain a constant flow of income that matched up with—or exceeded—monthly sales quotas.

She said, "Steve, that sounds like just what we need."

So it was then that we began teaching our internal system to outsiders. As of this writing, over 18,000 organizations have implemented the program, either through training administered by my company or through licensing arrangements. Many people who took the Prospect Management System training as salespeople over a decade ago are now sales managers who run their departments with the system outlined in this book.

As you will learn in the chapters that follow, the Prospect Management System is a *proven* method for managing your own activity, strategizing forward movement in the sales cycle, and *making more money.* It has stuck around for all these years for one simple reason: If you implement the system and feed it good information, it works. The Prospect Management System shows you exactly where you are now, what's on the horizon, and exactly what you need to focus on next with each individual prospect in order to hit your targets.

What follows is the simplest, most effective tool for helping salespeople that I've ever come across. I'd love to hear about your experiences with the system. Visit D.E.I. Management Group at <www.dei-sales.com>, or e-mail us at contactus@dei-sales.com, to share your thoughts on the Prospect Management System.

PART ONE

The Fundamentals

1

What You're Holding in Your Hands Increases Sales

The ideas in this book are part of a system that's been used successfully by hundreds of thousands of salespeople around the world. It is the number one process for increasing revenue by managing prospects effectively. It is also the very best process for permanently changing an organization's sales culture for the better.

The key to Getting to Closed™ is the Prospect Management System. This system has been:

- Implemented at companies like AT&T, Federal Express, Merrill Lynch, MCI/WorldCom, Sprint, Exxon-Mobil, Motorola, and Lexis-Nexis
- Successful in virtually all industries
- Licensed in North America, Latin America, and the Far East

The program you're holding in your hands right now is the single most effective program there is for increasing sales revenue tracking and maximizing relationships with prospects and customers.

> **REMEMBER THIS:** The Prospect Management System has been adopted at thousands of companies worldwide. It has been implemented successfully in virtually every industry.

We've gotten testimonials in praise of this program from salespeople in just about every industry you can name, but the one I want to share with you now is one that came our way recently from a salesperson in Austin, Texas. He wrote: "If you do what Steve Schiffman says, you will be successful."

I pass along that quote because I want to impress upon you the importance of *implementing what's here*. Practice new approaches to selling and strategizing. Don't adopt one or two parts of the program that feel familiar and try to use just those segments. Use it all, and you'll increase your income.

Follow all the instructions that appear in the main chapters of this book. Complete all the end-of-chapter tests. Make the principles in this book second nature in your selling routine. If you do this, you will be successful because the system will build in strategies that will *automatically* move your most important business relationships forward. That's my promise to you.

> **KEY POINT:** When implemented properly, the Prospect Management System will build key strategies into your selling day—strategies that will *automatically* move your most important business relationships forward.

Please complete the *Quick Quiz* for Chapter 1 before continuing with the next chapter.

QUICK QUIZ: CHAPTER 1

Please circle your answers.

1. The Prospect Management System has been successfully implemented . . .

    a. Throughout the greater Prince Edward Island area.
    b. In certain parts of Hoboken, New Jersey, the birthplace of legendary crooner Frank Sinatra.
    c. At thousands of companies, including many Fortune 1000 firms, located throughout North America, Europe, and Asia.
    d. None of the above.

2. For this program to work, you should . . .

    a. Read all the material through closely.
    b. Practice the strategies until they become second nature to you.
    c. Give new and unfamiliar approaches to selling and strategizing an honest try.
    d. All of the above.

3. When implemented properly, the Prospect Management System will build in key strategies to your selling day— strategies that will . . .

    a. Introduce you to new ways of manipulating prospects and customers into buying from you.
    b. *Automatically* help you move your most important business relationships forward.
    c. Build muscle mass and reduce unsightly fatty tissue in your upper body.
    d. None of the above.

Check your answers at the back of this book.

2

15, 7, and 1 (And Other Useful Insights on the Sales Process)

Every single day that I'm not training, I pick up the phone and make 15 dials. In other words, I call 15 companies I have never called before.

Out of these 15 dials, I typically complete the call to about seven of them—or, to look at it another way, I get through about half the time.

Out of those seven completed calls, I wind up setting one new appointment.

I do this every day I'm not in front of a group. What that means is that at the end of the week, I have set five brand new appointments. In a typical week, I go out on *eight* appointments: the five new appointments that I set, plus three appointments that have carried over from previous weeks. These typically are people I am seeing a second or third time.

Out of these eight appointments that I average every week, I typically close one sale per week.

Now if I do this every single week of the year, excluding the two weeks I take off for vacation, I sell something in the neighborhood of 50 new accounts.

15-7-1 each day = 5 new appointments per week
8:1 (closing ratio)
50 (total new accounts per year)

IMPROVING PERFORMANCE

Let's say I wanted to double my income. There are actually five ways I could go about doing that.

One way would be simply to double the number of dials I make. While that sounds sensible enough, the truth is that if I could have doubled the number of dials, if I could really be dialing 30 people a day instead of 15, I would probably already be doing that. Like most salespeople, I can't realistically expect to double my total dials because I will run out of time. (As a practical matter, the only salespeople I encounter who *could* double their dials are newcomers to the sales field who aren't really making enough calls to begin with.)

There are four other ways that I could (at least in theory) double my income. Each way involves actually monitoring and improving my ratios. Salespeople often talk about improving their numbers; my experience is that they make more progress when they take action to understand and improve their *ratios*.

> **REMEMBER THIS:** Selling is not a numbers game; selling is a ratios game.

So what's the first ratio I could improve? Well, it's possible that I could make the ratio between dials and completed calls better. If I got through to 14 people a day, instead of seven people a day, and if I still maintained the same number of calls every day, I could double my income. In fact, I've worked with salespeople who were able to change their approach and make just this kind of improvement.

Another ratio I could improve is the one between my completed calls and my total appointments. If I were averaging *two* appointments for every seven conversations, instead of just one, and if I averaged the same number of completed calls every single day throughout the course of a year, I would double my income.

The third ratio to look at is my closing ratio. If I closed two sales out of every eight appointments, instead of one out of eight, and if I still had the same number of total appointments over the course of the year, then I could double my income that way, too.

The final ratio I could use to improve my income is dollars to total sales. I could double my fee, or sell deeper into the account (that is, uncover new selling opportunities within an existing relationship) so that each sale is worth more to me. For example, if, on average, my typical sale was a one-day sales training program and I was able to move up to selling a two-day sales training program, I would double my income.

When all is said and done, there are really only five ways in sales we can actually improve our performance. Those five ways come down to increasing the number of total dials we make, or improving the four ratios I've just mentioned.

> **MANAGER'S RESOURCE:** If you ask your salespeople to monitor their own daily numbers and then make a habit of asking intelligent questions in each of the areas just discussed, you will see improvement in the ratios over time.

FOUR STEPS

Let's shift gears now and look at the selling process as a whole. Assume that the selling process has four steps. We use the diagram on the next page in our face-to-face training programs.

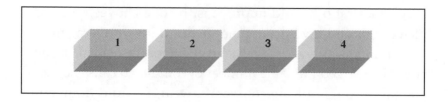

Given that there are four steps, what *has* to be the objective of the first step?

I've found that when I ask that question in a sales training program, many people will say, "Well, the objective is to get the appointment," or "The objective is to develop rapport," or "The goal is to get the other person to like you and trust you."

While all of that may sound right, the objective of the first step is really much simpler: *to get to the second step.*

Think about it. If selling has four steps (which it does), and you don't get to step two, you really don't have anything. So the goal of the first step simply has to be *to get to the second step.* If your first discussion ends with the contact saying, "Do me a favor; please don't ever come back!" then you really have nothing. You haven't moved forward to step two.

Let's follow that idea a little further. If the objective of step one is to get to step two, that would mean the objective of step two would be to get to step three. Similarly, the objective of step three would have to be to get to step four.

We can see, then, that the objective in every step of the sale is *simply to get to the next step.*

KEY POINT: The objective of any given step of the sale is simply to get to the next step.

You're probably wondering: What happens *within* each of the four steps? Well, let's work backwards through the steps and figure that out. The final step, the fourth step, would have to be the close—the point at which the person agrees to buy something from you.

Now to get a sale to close, you typically have to make a presentation or show the prospect your proposal. That means step number three is the presentation. We also call this step proposing a *plan* that makes sense to the prospect, but for now let's call it the *presentation*. (Please note for the record, however, that a presentation is *not* a demonstration! It's a customized plan based on unique information we've gathered about one particular prospect and his or her organization.)

How about step number two? In order to develop your presentation, in order to develop the plan that really makes sense to the other person, you have to gain and gather information. So let's call step two the *information-gathering* or interviewing step.

Prior to gaining and gathering information, you need to open up or qualify your sales call. That's what's happening in the first step.

Here are the four steps again with labels for each step.

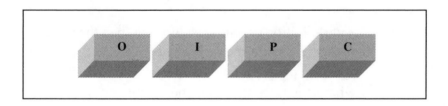

They are labeled with letters that identify them as opening, information gathering, presentation, and closing.

WHY YOU DON'T NEED TO FIND THE NEED

The critical step is that second one, information gathering.

At my company, we look at the information step very differently than some other companies do. Other sales trainers see the information step as a chance to find out what the prospect's needs are. But we believe that if the prospect really needed your product or your service, he or she would already have it!

Think about it. If a person really needed what you have to offer, wouldn't that person have taken some kind of action to call you up and try to get it?

We have a saying at D.E.I.: *People respond in kind.* That means that if you call someone up and ask, "Do you *need* our product and service?" or even, "Are you *interested* in so and so?" the chances are that that person would respond in kind. Probably, the answer you would get back would be, "No, I really don't *need* that," or, "No, I have absolutely no *interest* in that." However, if you were to call the person up and say, "What are you *doing* right now in such-and-such an area?" you would get an entirely differ-ent—response. You would have an entirely different—and, in all likelihood, far more constructive—conversation.

When you think about it, you realize the problem with need-based selling. Not enough people actually *need* our product and service when we *need* to make a sale! That's the big challenge I have with a sales approach that tries to find out what the other person needs.

At D.E.I., our definition of selling is different than the popular find-the-need formula. Instead of asking people what they need, we believe in asking people what they do, how they do it, when they do it, where they do it, whom they do it with, and why they're doing it that way.

When we've found out about all that, then—*and only then*—do we ask how we can help people do what they do better.

> **KEY POINT:** The definition of effective selling is *asking* people what they do, how they do it, when they do it, where they do it, whom they do it with, why they're doing it that way, and then helping them to do it better.

The key word in effective selling is not *need*, but *do*. The people we talk to may not need anything, but they are always doing something!

YOUR NUMBER ONE COMPETITOR

Your number one competitor is not a company. It's *the status quo.*

You have to get people to change what they are currently doing, and that means changing their habits. That's the real competition any salesperson faces.

Again: People don't *need* to change what they are currently doing, because what they are currently doing makes sense to them. How do we know that's true? Because whatever it is, they're still doing it!

This is an extremely important point. Let me share an illustration that may help clarify it. If you walked into someone's office and you saw a big brown cow standing in the corner chewing its cud, your first question to your contact would probably be, "Why do you have a brown cow in here?" Yet the average sales representative will walk into an appointment with a new contact, and when the person says, "Right now we are with the XYZ Company," the sales rep *will not ask about the brown cow*!

What do I mean by that? Well, the sales rep typically will *not* say, "Gee, I'm curious, why are you with the XYZ Company?" or, "Really? How did you choose to go with XYZ Company?" Such questions would illuminate the status quo, but the vast majority of salespeople don't ask those kinds of questions (or any meaningful questions). Instead, they look for the first opportunity to start regurgitating the material on their brochure.

We have to sell to the obvious, and that means *asking* about the obvious. That sounds simple enough, but it actually takes quite a bit of practice.

You'll find that that's the way it is with a lot of the information in this book. In order to change our results, we need to start looking at selling a little bit differently than we have looked at it in the past. If we keep doing exactly what we've done in the past, we are going to continue to get the same results.

USING QUESTIONS TO MOVE THE PROCESS FORWARD

Typically, salespeople *avoid* asking the questions that will move them through the sales cycle most effectively.

For instance, there is a very simple question we use at my company during an initial meeting with a new contact. This is a question that *instantly* identifies the status quo and launches the information-gathering step. Yet virtually all the salespeople we train are—at least at first—extremely hesitant about using it.

Here's what the question sounds like: "Mr. Smith, I checked my records and I noticed that you're not one of our customers. I'm just curious; why not?"

With a question like that, you instantly begin getting the information you want *and* you control the flow of the conversation. Remember: The questions you ask determine the direction and quality of the conversations you have.

Two of the most important kinds of questions to ask a prospect are *how* and *why* questions. By asking how and why a certain decision was made, the *who* emerges. You find out who the real decision maker is.

> **DO THIS:** Instead of asking "Who makes decisions in such-and-such an area?" ask "How did you decide to do so and so?" or "Why did you do it that way?" The answers you get will instantly point you toward *who* is actually making decisions.

TIME

As you go through each step in the sale, time is elapsing. But as it does, you're getting closer to your goal of 100 percent, or closure, with the people who are continuing to talk to you over whatever time span you're evaluating.

At my company, we happen to know that our sale, *on average,* takes about eight weeks. So if we are still working on a sale 28 weeks later, or 48 weeks later, or 98 weeks later, there's a problem.

I hope you'll agree that the chances of our getting the sale after 98 weeks certainly aren't as good as they were after eight weeks.

A related point about time is just as important to consider. The *longer* any given sale takes beyond its normal selling cycle, the *less* likely it is to close.

KEY POINT: Once a sale goes beyond its normal selling cycle, the odds of actually getting the business begin to drop.

What does that mean? It means that we can improve our performance if we spend *most* of our time interacting with prospects who haven't yet exceeded our time cycle.

THE FOUR STEPS REVISITED

Let's look at the four steps of the sales process once again. On the next page, each step is adjusted for size to reflect how much time we want to spend within that step.

Notice that the close is a tiny dot. That's an important point that most salespeople overlook. Typically, salespeople use the closing phase to unload all their closing tricks. They barrage the prospect with manipulative junk, then wonder why most people walk away.

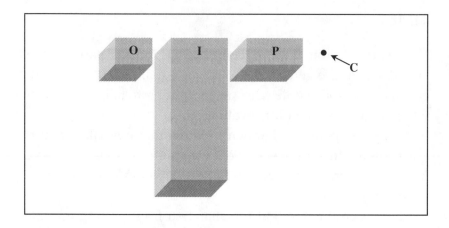

As a practical matter, we believe that the most effective way to close a sale is to turn to the prospect and say, "It makes sense to me, what do you think?" This only works, however, if your recommendation is based on sound information about what the prospect does.

> **DO THIS:** Before trying to close, ask yourself "Have I gathered all the relevant information?" If so, you can avoid those fancy "closing tricks" that don't really work. Next time you want to close a sale, simply say, "It makes sense to me, what do you think?"

When we use the "makes sense to me" closing strategy I've just described, what are we doing?

Actually, we're forcing the other person to *react*. It's a little bit like tossing a ball out to the prospect. He or she has to respond somehow. If the person catches the ball and tosses it back to us by saying, "Yes, it does make sense. When can we start?" then we know we've closed the sale. By the same token, the other person could also respond, "No, it doesn't make sense." Then we could ask, "Really? Why not?" Either way, we're going to get some kind of response.

When people tell us *why* what we've suggested doesn't make sense, what they will actually be telling us is what is wrong with our proposal. We want that information! By telling us what's wrong with our proposal, they're showing us how to make it right.

Here's another way to look at this extremely important point. The opposite of wrong is right and the opposite of right is wrong. That may seem self-evident, but look at what that simple idea actually means in practice: *In sales, we don't have to start out being right all the time. We simply need to be willing to be righted.* That "makes sense to me" close is a great way to get righted.

Actually, though *close* is really the wrong word for what's happening in the sale at this point. When you think about it, you're simply trying to get the prospect to decide to *use* your product or your service. Nothing is closing at all.

Because so many salespeople are used to referring to a formalization of a business deal as a close, I'm going to continue to use that term in this book. I want you to understand, however, that in the sales process, what's really happening is that the prospect is making a decision to *use* what we have to offer.

Please complete the *Quick Quiz* for Chapter 2 before continuing with the next chapter.

QUICK QUIZ: CHAPTER 2

Please circle your answers.

1. Selling is not a numbers game; selling is a _____ game.

    a. wicked
    b. ratios
    c. closing
    d. simple

2. What is the objective of the first step of the sales process?

    a. To get to the next step
    b. To build rapport
    c. To get the prospect to trust you
    d. To learn about the prospect's family

Check your answers at the back of this book.

3

Mastering the Sales Process

Let's look again at the four steps in the sales process.

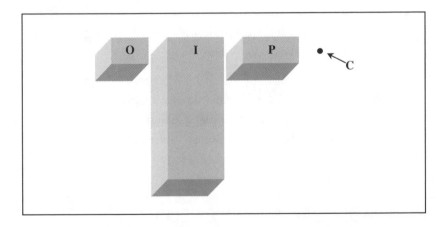

I noted in Chapter 2 that the second step is the critical one. Can you see why that is? In order to propose the right plan, the plan that's really going to make sense to the other person, we must first gain and gather the right information.

Notice the size of the information step in the previous illustration. It's by far the biggest step in the entire sale. The opening, by contrast, is relatively small. The information step represents most of the work in the sale. In fact, 75 percent of what you and I do as salespeople should happen *before* we make a formal presentation.

> **KEY POINT:** 75 percent of the work we do in the sales process must occur *before* we make a formal presentation.

Here's another interesting number to consider. My experience is that 90 percent of the presentations that fail to turn into revenue fail because they run into some kind of roadblock related to the second step. In other words, somewhere along the line, the salesperson missed an important piece of information during the information-gathering step of the process.

That makes sense, doesn't it? If the salesperson doesn't miss anything during that second step, and if he or she builds the plan around what the decision maker is actually trying to do, the proposal will probably make sense!

> **REMEMBER THIS:** If the information that we gather is complete, accurate, and on target, we're probably going to end up presenting a plan that will make sense to the prospect.

HOW MOST SALESPEOPLE SELL

Typically, salespeople sell according to the inefficient model shown at right.

They use a large opening that is usually gimmicky—a strained attempt to create some kind of rapport. "Nice furniture." "Nice desk." "Nice office." "You play golf?" "You go fishing?" And so on.

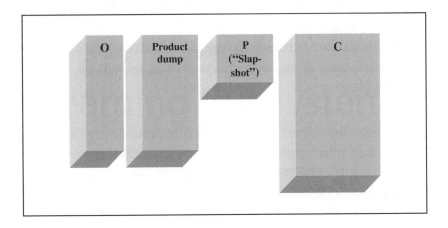

Then they start talking about the things with which they feel most comfortable—their product knowledge. In fact, they start *dumping* their product knowledge all over the prospect. We call this executing a product dump or throwing up on the prospect. Salespeople start to tell the prospect absolutely *everything* there is to know about their organization, about their product, about their service. Then when it suddenly dawns on them to ask a few questions, they start their presentation stage.

Instead of offering a plan that's based on what the prospect does, salespeople typically offer "slapshot" responses to the prospect's questions and comments. Every question or concern raised by the prospect receives an automatic answer, even though the salesperson hasn't asked any *meaningful* questions, such as: "What do you do? How do you do that? Who are your customers?"

What happens? Whenever the prospect says something like, "We're getting such and such from ABC Company," the salesperson responds instinctively, "Well, we have that too." Slapshot! We lose depth of information and have no platform from which to conduct the second step.

"You use 800 numbers? We have 800 numbers, too." "You use calling cards? We have calling cards, too." "You have roaming at no charge? Oh, we offer roaming at no charge, too."

> **KEY POINT:** Most salespeople simply give "slapshot" responses to counter whatever the prospect already has. They don't ask effective questions.

After playing "slapshot" for a while as part of a gigantic low-information presentation, most salespeople then try to find a way to actually close the sale, using one of those "187 can't-miss, sure-fire closing techniques."

You know the kind of techniques I'm talking about: old-fashioned closing tricks such as the roll-the-pen-across-the-table close ("Press hard, you're making six copies."), or the Ben Franklin close ("Let's make a list of all the advantages and disadvantages of buying and see which is longer.").

These tricks—and many others just as ineffective—have been outdated for a very long time, but somehow they still get used. Why? Because most salespeople simply feel uncomfortable saying something like, "Makes sense to me, what do you think?"

There's a reason salespeople feel uncomfortable saying that, of course. Deep down, they suspect their presentation never really made any sense to the prospect! Most of the time, they're right.

THE FOUR P'S

As salespeople, you and I need to be concerned with four things. I call them the Four P's: prospecting, presentation, product knowledge, and professional development.

Not long ago, we selected a group of 100 superior sales representatives. Each had to fit certain carefully chosen criteria.

Each person had to be working as a salesperson full time—not as a consultant, a marketing director, or anything else. Each one had to earn no less than $100,000 per year. (We did this to eliminate those people who had a good year simply because of a short-term change in the economy, a hot new product, or the inheritance of a good territory.)

In short, we selected a group of salespeople who could sell at high levels *consistently*, year in and year out. We tracked down 100 such salespeople and asked them about their working habits. What they told us was very interesting. We learned that

- 45 percent of their success came from their ability to prospect effectively.
- 20 percent of their success came from their ability to make an effective presentation.

So when you look at it, you realize that 65 percent of what you and I do as salespeople boils down to finding someone to talk to and then telling them what it is that we do.

Product knowledge, or product malleability as we call it at D.E.I., was another important factor. I could talk all day about product malleability, but this simply means taking a product and adapting it to fit what the customer is looking to do. This activity accounted for 20 percent of the success of the top salespeople we interviewed.

Finally, professional development—things the salespeople did to improve their own skills—accounted for the remaining 15 percent of their success.

So there you have it: the Four P's. These are four areas of activity worth considering closely if you want to succeed at the very highest levels.

THE ONE-THIRD RULE

Here's another benchmark for success to consider: the one-third rule.

This principle is pretty simple, but it carries many profound implications. Basically, it means that you're going to win approximately one-third of the total possible sales simply by showing up. If you showed up at enough accounts, introduced yourself, and simply passed along a brochure, you would eventually win *one-third* of those sales regardless of what else you did. Why? Who knows? You materialized at the perfect time. The decision maker was going on an overseas assignment and wanted to choose a vendor before leaving. The CEO said purchasing widgets was a time-sensitive priority. For whatever reason, you got the sale without any real effort. My experience is that anyone who's been selling for more than, say, a month and a half has had that experience of closing a sale that seemed to fall from the heavens.

By the same token, you're also going to *lose* one-third of your sales no matter what you do. Why? Basically, it's the same situation, only in reverse. Another salesperson showed up and offered something you couldn't match. The company suddenly announced a budget freeze. The leadership changed suddenly. These kinds of challenges also have happened to just about everyone who has sold for any amount of time.

What does all this mean? It means that the *middle third is up for grabs.* I'm talking about the one-third we could either win or lose depending on the skills we have as salespeople.

Our challenge is to develop a better selling routine than the competition, so we can get more of those sales that are in the up-for-grabs category. To make that happen, the question you have to ask yourself constantly is: *What can I do differently to change the results I'm getting?* The answer, as you'll see a little later in this book, is to manage your prospect base intelligently.

20:5:1

At D.E.I., we have trained roughly half a million salespeople over more than two decades. That's a lot of experience, and we've used it to develop some interesting yardsticks.

Here's one of the most helpful standards we've developed based on our interviews with salespeople. We've found that, as a broad but very reliable rule, 20 cold calls typically will yield five prospects, and five prospects typically will yield one sale. There's some slight variation on those numbers from company to company and industry to industry, but in general those numbers do tend to hold firm.

Here's the interesting part. In a training program, we will say to sales representatives, "Look at these ratios: 20 calls gives us five prospects that lead to one sale. How many 'no' answers do you see?"

You'd be surprised at the variety of the answers we get. In fact, it takes 19 "no" answers to generate that one sale.

So here's my question: Why do salespeople seem to go out of their way to avoid those "no" answers?

COUNT THE "NO" ANSWERS

Amazingly, most sales representatives never even count the "no" answers that they generate. They know the number of sales they made last week, or last month, or last quarter. They know what the total on their W-2 was, what their base salary is, and what their commission percentage is. They even know how many miles it takes to drive to the office. But if I ask them how many companies they have to call to generate a single sale, they stare at me as though I'm speaking to them in Swahili.

If you don't know how many "no" answers it takes you to get a sale, then you will never know whether you are getting enough "no" answers on a given day, or during a given week, or over the course of a quarter!

Count the "no" answers. Each and every one of those "no" answers is actually worth money to you. The question is, of course, how *much* money? You'll have to monitor your own numbers to get the answer to that question, but I can assure you that there is a dollar figure that will get your attention somewhere along the line. In fact, one of our clients actually paid salespeople a bonus after they racked up a certain number of rejections from prospects!

As it happened, that was a tremendously successful program. The reason: It dramatically drove home a key point. *If all you do is count "yes" answers, you'll never know how many "no" answers make a single sale possible!*

WHAT HAPPENS WHEN YOU DON'T PROSPECT FOR NEW BUSINESS?

Let's assume that your sales cycle is similar to ours, and that you have an eight-week selling cycle. In other words, suppose it typically takes you eight weeks to move from your first contact with someone to closing the sale with that person.

Let's suppose that today is January 1. If you go out on an appointment today, you will close eight weeks later, which would be on March 1.

But suppose you *did not* have a first appointment today. No first appointment with anyone at all would mean that on March 1, you *would not* have a sale.

Unfortunately, you cannot make up for lost time. If you don't have a new sales appointment on January 1, January 2, or January 3, your income also moves back—day by day. If you were to go an entire *week* without making a new appointment and initiating a new contact, you'd see a drop in income, because your sale wouldn't close until March 8!

You're not going to feel a drop in sales immediately. (After all, your selling cycle is eight weeks.) But I guarantee you that you *are* going to notice the sales drop eight weeks later.

This leads to an interesting series of questions. When did you actually earn the money you're making today? Eight weeks ago!

If you have no new appointment today, what are your chances of getting a new prospect today? Zero!

If you have no prospect today, what are your chances of making a sale today? Zero!

Take a look at this formula.

$$A_{>}P_{>S}$$

A stands for appointments, *P* stands for prospects, and *S* stands for sales. Understanding this principle is the key to what I call *Active Prospect Selling,* which is what makes Getting to Closed possible.

A lot of first appointments leads to a smaller number of prospects, which leads to a smaller number of sales. If we don't keep restocking that appointments category, we lose ground and we end up having to struggle to make up lost ground.

Typically, salespeople have a good week, followed by a bad week; a good month, followed by a bad month; a good quarter, followed by a bad quarter. Why is this cycle so common? In virtually every case, it's because, at some point, they've lost sight of that *A* category: initial appointments. When this happens there's an income crisis, and a very stressful catch-up period. This stressful peaks-and-valleys income cycle ends up looking something like this:

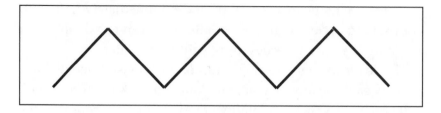

Is it necessary? Not if you master your ratios and attend to them on a daily basis. We ask the sales reps we train to consider the following question: "If you had 100 prospects, would you expect all 100 to close?"

Usually, the answer we get is, "Of course not. I'll only close a fraction of those." We find that the fraction people typically close is roughly one-fifth—one out of five of our prospects turns into a sale. (This is consistent with our 20:5:1 ratio.)

So we know that it takes approximately five active prospects to yield a single sale. As we go around the United States and around the world doing our training programs, we typically find that sales reps are working on no more than about 20 prospects at any given time. That's all they can realistically handle.

Now, think back to that peaks-and-valleys pattern. When a sales rep who has 20 prospects makes one sale, the salesperson *thinks* he or she has 19 prospects left. But if you recall our one-in-five closing ratio, you realize that there are really far fewer than that.

Because each and every sale I make requires five prospects, I should really think of my prospect base as having 14 prospects because, statistically, four prospects are going to disappear eventually, regardless of their current status. This is a very important point!

KEY POINT: If your closing ratio is 5-to-1, then every sale you make must be replenished by *five* new prospects—not one—if your prospect base is to remain full.

Confused? Follow me through this chain of reasoning for just a moment. If I started out with 20 prospects and I made one sale, I *wouldn't* really have 19 left, which is what most salespeople would think they had. I would have, in fact, 15 left . . . because my 5-to-1 closing ratio dictates that that's all I could realistically expect to count on for income, which is what really matters.

Follow me so far? Good. Now consider the implications. If I made one more sale and I were the average salesperson, I might think that there were 18 prospects left, but, in fact, I would really only have ten. If I made another sale, it might seem to me as though I had 17 prospects left, when, in fact, I would only have five. If I made a fourth sale without replenishing my prospect base in any way, I would actually have no reliable prospects left, although I might be tempted to think that I have 16.

Here's the bottom line. If I make the mistake of ignoring the task of constantly replenishing my prospect base, or if I prospect intermittently, but fool myself into believing that I can replace one sale with *just one* new prospect, I'll be in trouble. I'll wake up one morning and realize that my 16 prospects are suddenly down to zero. (This will only seem sudden if I haven't been doing my job. I should have seen the crisis coming!)

When every single one of these former prospects has finally—and predictably—said no to me, what am I likely to do? Well, if I'm like most salespeople, I'll panic. After I knock that little item off the to-do list, I'll probably go into crisis management mode and I'll start prospecting like crazy in a feverish attempt to make up for the time I've squandered. I'll knock myself out to build my base back up to 20 or so legitimate prospects, but as soon as I've done that, the whole cycle will repeat until I finally realize that my prospect base must be continually replenished in a way that supports my own closing ratio.

THE MOST IMPORTANT QUESTION

The critical daily question we face in sales is actually a pretty simple one. What's the right number of appointments that we should be maintaining at all times?

We have to take daily action to maintain a consistent level of sales and avoid the ups and downs in the sales process. *The key to success in selling is managing our own base of prospects intelligently and consistently.*

KEY POINT: If you manage your base of prospects effectively, you will be successful.

Please complete the *Quick Quiz* for Chapter 3 before continuing with the next chapter.

QUICK QUIZ: CHAPTER 3

Please circle your answers.

1. Which of the following statements best reflects the role of the "no" answer in your sales work?

   a. A prospect who says no to me is one who hasn't yet learned about how I can help him or her meet key needs.
   b. A prospect who says no to me means that, for that organization, I haven't done my job as a salesperson.
   c. A prospect who says no to me is one of the many "no" answers I need to generate a single "yes" answer and is an essential part of generating that "yes" response.
   d. None of the above.

2. In an ideal sales cycle, how much of the work should come before you make a presentation?

   a. 75 percent
   b. 10 percent
   c. 50 percent
   d. None of the above.

3. The key to success in selling is . . .

   a. Developing an arsenal of effective closing tricks.
   b. Saying flattering things about the prospect's family during initial meetings.
   c. Managing and maintaining your base of prospects effectively.
   d. None of the above.

Check your answers at the back of this book.

4

Common Questions about the Sales Process

*H*ow *can I possibly estimate what my average selling cycle is? Some accounts do take longer to close than others, don't they?*

This is a little like asking, "How can anyone say what the average height of a 30-year-old American man is? Some men are taller than others, aren't they?" It's true. Some 30-year-old men are short. Others are tall. But there is an average.

You do have an average selling cycle. The only question is whether or not you've identified it.

When we ask people during our training sessions to tell us what their average selling cycle is, we hear a lot of this kind of response: "Well, it varies." Of course it varies! That's why we go to the trouble of adding the numbers together and dividing them—to take account of that variance and use it to generate a meaningful estimate of the length of time it takes to close a sale.

Your average selling cycle is just that: an average. You can determine it by analyzing your most recent 20 or 30 sales and identifying how long each took to complete. Add up all the figures and divide by the number of sales you're analyzing. The answer you get *is* your average selling cycle, even though some sales definitely do take longer than others.

Having identified the average selling cycle, you must ask yourself: How can I use what I know about your cycle to sell more intelligently? Your answer to this question can have a dramatic positive impact on your career as a salesperson. Consider the following true story.

Recently, we worked with a company that closed significantly more than half of its sales—70 percent, to be precise—during its first phone call with a prospect. It closed about a quarter of its sales on the second phone call, and it closed the remainder of its sales on the third call. Virtually nothing closed on the fourth call.

In such a setting, it's not *impossible* to sell someone on the second call, but it's certainly far less likely than selling them on the first call. So does it really make sense to call a lead for a fourth, fifth, sixth, or seventh time? Of course not!

That's why we advised telemarketers at that organization to stop making that fourth call. Instead, they were to use the available time to reach out to new prospects. The result: Sales skyrocketed!

Understand what happened here. Simply by focusing its efforts on prospects who fell within its sales cycle, the company was able to dramatically increase its income. Everything else stayed the same!

You can begin to see the incredible potential of managing your time effectively during your interactions with prospects. The same principle applies to face-to-face selling, and can have equally dramatic results. (Another company we worked with increased its face-to-face appointments by 670 percent by implementing essentially the same ideas.)

If you are a face-to-face salesperson, I challenge you to analyze your numbers. You will find that the vast majority of your sales take place by X number of weeks after the first meeting with the prospect. Once you identify what X is, work with that number! If you know that 80 percent of your customers sign with you after two weeks, don't make it your top time priority to meet with people who have been in your base for seven or eight weeks.

DO THIS: Analyze your numbers. Know your selling cycle. Avoid wasting time and energy on prospects who have gone well beyond that selling cycle without buying.

My industry and selling environment is unique. Isn't there some rationale for my focusing exclusively on closing imminent business—and skipping prospecting—for just a few days?

No. Strictly speaking, of course, *every* industry is unique. *Every* selling environment has distinctive elements. But *no* industry and *no* selling environment that we've ever come across is exempt from what we call the Law of Replacement. If it takes you eight prospects to deliver one sale, then every sale you register means you must replenish your base with eight new prospects.

The problem with skipping prospecting for just a few days is that it tends to become a habit—a habit that superstar performers resolutely avoid.

DO THIS: Prospect daily and follow the Law of Replacement by replenishing your prospect base with a number that reflects your actual closing ratio. (That number will be more than one!)

How do I know which prospects to focus my attention on?

By using the Prospect Management System. Now that you understand the four phases of the selling cycle, you're ready to learn how to put the system to work. You'll begin doing that in Part Two of this book.

The Prospect Management System uses a special date-driven tracking system that allows you to monitor and rank all your sales opportunities. By using this tool, you can rank contacts according to how likely each one is to close.

This system *forces* you to be realistic about your prospects and recategorize contacts that aren't active.

If you use the Prospect Board correctly, you will never again fall into the trap of focusing exclusively on current business or on potential business that cannot be entered on your calendar in the form of a face-to-face meeting.

The Prospect Board you'll be reading about in Part Two can be a magnetic setup, a personal portfolio with plenty of slots for cards, a simple bulletin board you can put together on your own, or a copy printed from our Web-based Prospect Management software, as shown below (visit <www.dei-sales.com> to learn more).

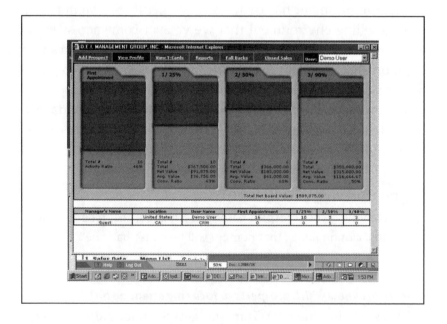

Many of the companies we work with use the software or purchase a large magnetic board from us. They then use these tools to track the activity of a department or company as a whole; they also encourage the individual reps to track their own activity by means of smaller personal portfolios, which are regularly incorporated into the results of the team as a whole.

However you implement the system, what matters is that you implement it. You can certainly get exemplary results with the low-tech approach (using a marker, a big bulletin board, and a stack of three-by-five cards). This is a matter of personal style and corporate culture more than anything else. For more information on ordering our company's Prospect Management equipment or software, contact D.E.I. Management Group at 800-224-2140.

REMEMBER THIS: Your Prospect Board—whether homemade, ordered via D.E.I., or managed on a laptop with D.E.I. software—is your key to strategizing and managing your sales activity.

Is the Prospect Management System organized specifically around the four steps of the sales cycle?

It goes even further than that.

As you'll see when you learn about the various groupings for prospects and contacts, the Prospect Management System uses a somewhat deeper level of analysis to help you break your contacts into *six* major categories. Most of the interesting and important sales work, as you have seen, takes place during the second step—interviewing. The Prospect Management System is set up in such a way to give you plenty of information about exactly what's going on in that step.

KEY POINT: The Prospect Management System gives you a snapshot of your sales activity throughout the cycle and provides close-ups of what's actually happening during the crucial second step (information gathering) of the sales cycle.

Please complete the *Quick Quiz* for Chapter 4 before continuing with the next chapter.

QUICK QUIZ: CHAPTER 4

Please circle your answers.

1. Prospecting every working day is . . .

    a. Mandatory.
    b. A good idea if you've got the time.
    c. Unimportant.
    d. Recommended, but not mandatory.

2. The number of new prospects you must reintroduce to your base after closing a sale is . . .

    a. One.
    b. More than one.
    c. Less than one.
    d. Unimportant.

3. Your Prospect Board can be . . .

    a. A magnetic setup.
    b. A personal portfolio with plenty of slots for cards.
    c. A simple bulletin board you put together on your own.
    d. Tracked with D.E.I. software.
    e. All of the above.

Check your answers at the back of this book.

5

Monitoring Your Numbers

Three letters can change your career.

The three letters are the very ones you learned about in Chapter 3:

$$A >\!P _{>S}$$

As you recall, in this equation a large number of appointments leads to a smaller number of prospects, which leads to a smaller number of sales.

This sequence is vitally important. So important that it's worth reviewing closely. Again, lots of appointments lead to a smaller number of prospects, which in turn lead to an even smaller number of sales. Too often, we focus only on the final element. We count only the "yes" answers—the sales—without considering how many appointments began the process, or how much work it took to get someone into the active prospect category. As you've seen, we often forget that people drop out of the process along the way.

Let's illustrate this very important point briefly, in real numbers, as it relates to a real, live salesperson.

Ten first appointments might turn into *three* active prospects. By active prospects, I mean people who continue to "play ball" with us by agreeing to some kind of next step. (You'll learn more about the formal definition of a prospect in Chapter 6.) These three active prospects might turn into *one* sale.

KEY POINT: If you want the one sale, you have to be willing to set the ten appointments and move those contacts through the sales process, because A>P>S.

IT'S UP TO YOU

Only you can monitor and manage your sales numbers. You can't rely on your sales manager to do it for you.

If it takes you 60 dials to generate four appointments, and it takes you four appointments to generate one active prospect, *you* have to be the person who asks the tough questions: How many active prospects do I need to have to meet my income goals? What do I have to do to get that many prospects?

Your sales manager may or may not ask that question, but you *must* ask it—and answer it! You must do the math and set the goals for yourself.

The numbers in the following example are not your numbers, so studying them can't really be considered a substitute for monitoring your own numbers. But studying these numbers is a good way to master the process of monitoring sales activity and strategizing goals.

Look closely at these numbers.

✓ My income goal: $75,000
✓ My average commission per sale: $3000
✓ Sales I need over the course of a year: 25
✓ Dials needed to generate a single appointment: 15
✓ Appointments needed to generate a single active prospect (second meeting): 4
✓ Active prospects needed to generate a single sale: 6
✓ Total active prospects I must develop over the course of a year: 150 (6 × 25)
✓ Total appointments I must set to generate that many active prospects over the course of a year: 600 (4 × 150)
✓ Total dials I must make to generate that many appointments over the course of a year: 9000
✓ Working days in my year: 250
✓ Average number of dials I must make each working day to hit my income goal: 36 (9000 ÷ 250)

Now that you've seen the process for yourself, take the plunge. Use a form like the one below to establish your own income goal and your own daily activity requirement.

✓ My income goal: _____
✓ My average commission per sale: _____
✓ Sales I need over the course of a year: _____
✓ Dials needed to generate a single appointment: _____
✓ Appointments needed to generate a single active prospect (second meeting): _____
✓ Active prospects needed to generate a single sale: _____
✓ Total active prospects I must develop over the course of a year: _____
✓ Total appointments I must set to generate that many active prospects over the course of a year: _____
✓ Total dials I must make to generate that many appointments over the course of a year: _____
✓ Working days in my year: _____
✓ Average number of dials I must make each working day to hit my income goal: _____

Did you fill in all the blanks? I hope so. If you're a salesperson, you *must* master this process yourself. I wish I could do it for you. I wish you could rely on your sales manager to do it for you. The hard truth is that it really is all up to you.

If you track the numbers, you can figure out how many dials you actually have to make to generate a single sale, and how many you have to make each day to hit your income goal for the year.

Before we close this chapter and move forward to Part Two of this book, let me share an important point. I believe that success in selling *will come* if you prospect well.

If for some reason you only have mediocre selling skills but you have great prospecting skills, you really will be fine. Your closing activity will start to take care of itself and you'll make a good living.

But you can't, in my experience, do it the other way around. If you have great interpersonal, interviewing, and presentation skills, but you *can't* prospect effectively and track your numbers, you will not be successful.

With that in mind, let's move on to the heart of the book. Once you complete the end-of-chapter quiz, you'll be ready to get acquainted with the Prospect Management Board.

Please complete the *Quick Quiz* for Chapter 5 before continuing with the next chapter.

QUICK QUIZ: CHAPTER 5

Please circle your answer.

1. Ultimate responsibility for setting and monitoring daily selling activity resides with . . .

   a. You.
   b. Your sales manager.
   c. Your colleagues.
   d. All of the above.

Check your answer at the back of this book.

PART TWO

Learning the System

6

Don't Wait for No

What do we know for sure now? Well, we know that if we do the first 75 percent of our job correctly by opening the relationship and gathering information, and the person is still "playing ball" with us—that is, agreeing to continue discussions—then our presentation will make sense. We will more than likely close the sale. Our "close" equals the other person's decision to *use* what we have to offer.

KEY POINT: Close = Use.

Our objective, then, is to spend as much of our time as possible playing ball with the people who want to play ball with us. That means we have to recognize when someone is playing ball with us and, just as important, when someone isn't.

THE NEXT STEP

What you're about to read may seem strange, but it is nevertheless true. The single best predictor of success in implementing an effective prospect management strategy is a willingness *not* to talk to certain people.

Let me explain what I mean. We've trained nearly half a million salespeople over the years, and we've noticed a striking thing. The people who turn into superstars, the ones who learn to sell at peak efficiency, are the ones who decide to become very selective about who gets their time, attention, and energy after initial contact has been made.

Specifically, the salespeople I'm talking about—the ones who achieve at the very highest levels—severely limit the amount of time they spend with people who are *not* prospects.

At D.E.I., we use a very narrow definition of the word *prospect*. Whenever we talk about a prospect, we're talking about someone who has proved by his or her actions to be willing to discuss various products and services. This person is therefore moving through the steps of the sales process with you.

KEY POINT: A prospect is someone who agrees to go through the sales process with you.

You'll recall that appointments lead to prospects, which lead to sales, and that each group is progressively smaller in size. In other words, the further along you are at any given point of the sales cycle, the greater the number of prospects who will drop out, but the more likely you are to close with those who remain. (Remember, too, the other conclusion we came to: the longer any given sale goes beyond the length of your typical sale, the less likely you are to close that person.)

The vitally important point—the point that may determine your success or failure as a salesperson—is that *not everyone you talk to will be a prospect!*

> **KEY POINT:** Not everyone you talk to is a prospect!

IS IT A PROSPECT OR IS IT AN OPPORTUNITY?

Too many salespeople believe they have assembled a large number of prospects, when in fact they have assembled contacts in other categories. They waste their time, effort, and energy on people who have already demonstrated, either actively or passively, that they are *not* interested in playing ball.

There are a number of categories for the people with which you come in contact. "Prospect" is only *one* of those categories.

Don't make the common mistake of considering absolutely everyone you encounter a prospect. To succeed at the highest level, you're going to have to identify, strategize, and manage your actual prospects—and put other contacts on the back burner. If you're not defining people correctly, your income will suffer.

There is a name we can use to describe the people with which we *want* to work but who are *not* yet actively playing ball with us. We call these people *opportunities.*

> **KEY POINT:** Most salespeople believe they have assembled a large number of prospects, when, in fact, they have assembled a large number of opportunities.

There are a number of subcategories within the "opportunities" category. Here's how those subcategories break down.

Candidates

A *candidate* is a possible user, choice, or nominee for your service. For instance, if you know that I could use what you have to offer, but you have not yet gotten me to agree to some kind of next step with you, then I am a candidate within your group of opportunities.

Suspects

A *suspect* is a person or organization you have reason to believe could be a candidate for your service. If you do not yet know for certain that I could use what you have to offer, but you *suspect* I could, and you have not yet gotten me to agree to some kind of next step with you, then I am a suspect within your group of opportunities.

Leads

A *lead* is a person or organization that has contacted your firm. Leads may also arise from a response to an advertisement or promotion. If I receive one of your company's direct mail pieces and then leave a voice message requesting more information, I am a lead within your opportunity base.

> **KEY POINT:** If your contact hasn't made any kind of commitment to you, you don't have a prospect. You have an opportunity.

Referrals

A *referral* is someone you've heard about through your own active network of contacts, but who hasn't begun to move through the sales process with you. If one of your current customers suggests that you contact me about your product or service, but you and I have not yet spoken, then I am a referral within your opportunity base.

OPPORTUNITIES ARE GREAT!

Does it *ever* make sense to contact opportunities directly? Of course! That's part of the prospecting process. That's how you initiate new business.

Does it make sense to spend *all* of your time calling and recalling opportunities, when you could be moving relationships forward with actual prospects? No!

The aim is always to find out what level of commitment really exists with any given contact, and how that commitment reflects your likelihood of closing with that person.

Unfortunately, it's easy to fool ourselves into thinking we're talking to a prospect when we really aren't. But to make the Prospect Management System work, we have to be ruthlessly honest with ourselves about the level of commitment that exists.

For instance:

- Someone who ends a conversation by suggesting you call at some vague point in the future is *not* a prospect.
- Someone who told you last month that she was very interested in talking about your company but won't take your call now is *not* a prospect.
- Someone who tells you he will be willing to talk about working with your company after talking things over with others in the organization, but won't commit to a time for a follow-up call is *not* a prospect.

No matter how well the conversation goes, no matter how pleasant your contact is, if there is no next step, no sign of a commitment to work through the cycle with you, you're not going to classify that organization as a prospect.

DON'T WAIT TO HEAR NO TO KNOW WHAT YOU'VE GOT!

Often, salespeople wait to hear the word *no* before they take a contact out of the "prospect" category. The truth is, a person can "say no" to you in many ways, including:

- Failing to return phone calls
- Asking that you call back in six weeks (or six months)
- Telling you he or she is planning to discuss your company with the president next week

Once you recognize these signals for what they are, you can accurately classify the level of commitment from your prospects and customers. That means you can:

- Maximize your chance of closing
- Work with the right number of prospects
- Avoid a drop in sales and income
- Maintain the right numbers of prospects in specific categories

By using the Prospect Management System to categorize your contacts into six specific groups, you will gain deeper insight into your own typical sales cycle. You'll learn exactly where you're having difficulty, and you'll get a better idea about what they should be doing to correct things. You'll be continually reminded of the main jobs you face as a salesperson: keeping the appointments coming, and moving as many prospects as you can along to the next stage.

Once you familiarize yourself with all six of the categories and learn to use them on a daily basis, you'll be able to focus your attention *automatically* on your most important business relationships. Later on in this book, you'll learn to use the categories to forecast your income more effectively than you're probably doing right now. Most important, you'll learn how to make the roller coaster income swings most salespeople constantly contend with a thing of the past by managing your first appointments category intelligently.

The system you'll learn about in this section of the book allows you to assume personal control of your sales work and evaluate exactly where you are at any moment. If you use it each and every day, you'll know how your prospecting efforts will eventually pay off, and you'll also have a tangible reminder of where you stand with each individual lead in your prospect base.

Please complete the *Quick Quiz* for Chapter 6 before continuing with the next chapter.

QUICK QUIZ: CHAPTER 6

Please circle your answers.

1. Someone who says, "This sounds interesting. Send me some information and give me a call sometime next quarter" is . . .

   a. A prospect.
   b. An opportunity.
   c. None of the above.

2. "My boss can't take your call now and I'm not allowed to let you leave a message. Why don't you call back sometime next week. Things won't be so busy then, and he'll be able to listen to what you have to say." This company is . . .

   a. A prospect.
   b. An opportunity.
   c. None of the above.

3. "This has been a good meeting. I'd like for both of us to meet with our VP of Finance next Thursday at 2:00 so we can see where to go from here." This person is . . .

   a. A prospect.
   b. An opportunity.
   c. None of the above.

Check your answers at the back of this book.

7

The Opportunity Column

In this chapter, you'll begin to become familiar with the six categories of the Prospect Management System, shown below.

THE PROSPECT MANAGEMENT SYSTEM CATEGORIES

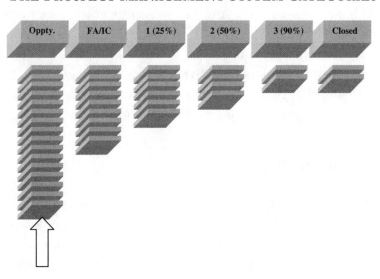

Reading from left to right we have columns for opportunities, first appointments (or initial contacts for those selling in a telemarketing environment), 25 percent prospects, 50 percent prospects, 90 percent prospects, and closed.

We will discuss each of the groups in depth individually in this chapter and the chapters that follow. The first category we will become familiar with is the one on the far left-hand side marked "opportunities."

The classifications you will begin studying now are the heart of the Prospect Management System; they are extremely easy to use. *You cannot get any benefit from the system if you do not become familiar with the categories.*

> **DO THIS:** Become intimately familiar with the simple classification criteria discussed in Chapters 7 through 12 of this book. Be sure you complete all the relevant end-of-chapter exercises!

If you use the criteria of this system to evaluate and maintain your base of prospects, you will even out your sales performance and be able to maintain it at a high level that is consistent and makes sense for you.

The Prospect Management System uses six categories to give you a "snapshot" of the business you're currently developing. It helps you categorize *everything* you're working on.

A KEY PRINCIPLE

Please remember the key point from Chapter 6. A prospect is someone who is willing to discuss your products or services with you, and who *proves that willingness* by scheduling a meeting or other next step with you to discuss potential business. Your goal is to move the prospect through the various steps of the process.

If a prospect isn't playing ball with you—working with you to move forward to the next stage in the cycle—then there's a problem. I cannot emphasize that point enough!

We know that not everyone you prospect will move on to the interviewing phase with you. We know that not everyone you interview will move on to presentation stage with you. We know that not everyone you present to will commit to buy from you. We also know that if you don't have a sizeable base of first appointments, you won't have enough prospects moving forward through the various stages of sales cycle!

Opportunities—the group we're focusing on now—aren't prospects yet. They're not even appointments. They're the people or companies we *want* to do business with. They could be people or companies we haven't called. They could also be people or companies we've talked to in the past, but currently have no active discussions with about potential business.

> **KEY POINT:** Use the opportunities column to keep track of those people you want to do business with, but who have not yet committed to a next step.

Please, for the sake of your own career, remember what I've shared with you: A contact that hasn't made any kind of commitment to you *is not a prospect*! That person is an opportunity and belongs in the far left-hand column of your Prospect Board. We may also refer to people in this group as fallbacks, because contacts from other columns sometimes fall back to this column when there is no evidence of action or commitment.

> **MANAGER'S RESOURCE:** Constantly remind your salespeople that "great calls" or "great visits" without a committed next step translate into *opportunities,* not active prospects. Track the number of true prospects they have at all times.

The objective in the opportunity column is always to move the contact forward to one of the other categories.

The opportunity column is a great place to "park" dormant contacts that have exceeded the average limits of your sales cycle.

At least three good things can arise from fallbacks or opportunities:

1. You devote more energy to prospects who *are* progressively moving through the steps.
2. You have the chance to take time to strategize with managers and colleagues on a better way to "get involved" with these companies.
3. You are more likely to take immediate action when there's a problem. After all, if you hadn't reclassified the contact, you might not have been as motivated to take action.

Please complete the *Quick Quiz* for Chapter 7 before continuing with the next chapter.

QUICK QUIZ: CHAPTER 7

Please circle your answers.

1. The opportunity column is an active prospect category.

   a. True
   b. False

2. A contact has met with you a number of times and has made it clear that the president of the company, with whom you have been unable to meet, is the sole decision maker when it comes to purchase decisions involving your product. Your contact is willing to set appointments to discuss technical matters, but cannot provide you with any access

to the CEO. After three meetings, you have been asked to call back next month. Which of the following descriptions best fits this situation?

a. Opportunity/Fallback
b. Prospect
c. None of the above.

3. A contact who falls back from an active prospect category cannot move forward again.

a. True
b. False

Check your answers at the back of this book.

8

The Closed Column

At the other end of the Prospect Board is the closed column.

THE PROSPECT MANAGEMENT SYSTEM CATEGORIES

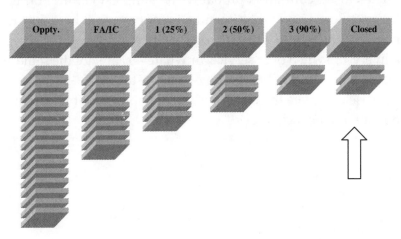

We know what that group is. These are the people or companies who've decided to buy from us.

They've made a commitment to *use* what we have to offer. This is confirmed business, but, of course, the people in this column may also represent additional opportunities for new or increased sales.

In the closed column, the deal is done and the contract is signed. Actually, though, a contract may or may not be the measure you use to determine when a business relationship begins. Some of the businesses we work with call an account "closed" when:

- The first payment has been received
- Commission has been paid
- Delivery has been fulfilled
- Service has been switched over

Whatever measure you use to determine when a prospect becomes a customer, use it consistently. Only place people in the closed column who meet your standard in this area.

The closed column is probably the simplest column on the Prospect Board, so I won't spend a lot of time on it here. Just remember that people who tell you they're *about* to pay (or accept delivery, or switch over service, or whatever) are not the same as people who actually *have* become your customers.

Please complete the *Quick Quiz* for Chapter 8 before continuing with the next chapter.

QUICK QUIZ: CHAPTER 8

Please circle your answer.

1. An active prospect tells you he's very interested in working with you, and wants to sign on as soon as the committee gives this the "rubber stamp." This person belongs in the closed category.

   a. True
   b. False

Check your answer at the back of this book.

9

The First Appointment Column

mmediately to the right of the opportunities column is the first appointment column. This is for people with whom we've scheduled an upcoming initial appointment. We haven't yet met with them.

THE PROSPECT MANAGEMENT SYSTEM CATEGORIES

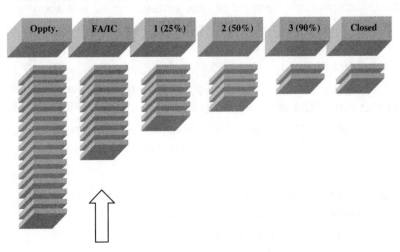

KEY POINT: When we make a first appointment, our contact moves out of the opportunity category and into the first appointment (or FA) category.

AN ADAPTATION FOR THE TELEMARKETING ENVIRONMENT

Many salespeople work in a telemarketing selling environment. For them, identifying whether a first appointment to meet personally has been set is not appropriate. That's why this column can also be called the initial contact category.

For a telemarketing sales professional, a contact moves out of the opportunity category and into the initial contact category upon the completion of the second good call. You know intuitively what a good call is, I'm sure, but let me explain it here for the sake of thoroughness.

It's relatively easy to reach a new decision maker on the phone and have a single productive conversation. (For advice on how to do just this, please see my book *Telesales*, 2nd ed. Adams Media, 2002.) During that first call, you can, with a little practice, reach a respectable number of new contacts, pose just about any question, and get some kind of positive—or at least vaguely interested—response. *That response, however, does not turn the person into an initial contact.*

Only at the end of the *second* productive call do we move the contact out of the opportunity column. Once the person has decided to take our call and talk to us for a second time, then we have persuasive evidence of an emerging relationship.

REMEMBER THIS: Initial contacts are the telemarketing equivalent of scheduled first appointments. One good conversation does *not* constitute initial contact!

Again, this standard is only of interest to those who close sales over the phone for a living. For salespeople who do most of their business in a face-to-face setting, the act of scheduling a first appointment is a sufficient signal of interest to move the person out of the opportunity column.

A NOTE ON TERMINOLOGY

From the standpoint of board management, it doesn't matter whether you're a telemarketer tracking initial contacts or a field salesperson tracking first appointments. Whatever you call them, the people who land in this column have changed their routine for you; they've expressed interest in establishing a business relationship. That's what's really important.

For simplicity, I'm going to refer to this column as the first appointment or FA column from this point forward in the book, even though the principles we'll be discussing are applicable both to field salespeople and telemarketing professionals.

FAS DRIVE THE SALES PROCESS

The all-important A>P>S formula we examined earlier means appointments lead to prospects and prospects lead to sales, but it could also be translated, in practical terms, as FAs drive your sales process.

The first appointment column is not technically considered an active prospect column, but it is nevertheless a very important column. In fact, it may be the most important one on the board. Why? Because your job as a salesperson is to determine, through analyzing your ratios, how many appointments you need in order to bring in the sales you require and *maintain this column at that level at all times*!

Because your relationship with your contact is still unfolding, the FA column is not considered an active prospect category. Yet maintaining a consistent and appropriate level of FAs on your board is probably the most important step in implementing the Prospect Management System.

KEY POINT: Maintaining a consistent and appropriate level of FAs is probably the single most important step in implementing the Prospect Management System. You must know *exactly* how many FAs support your income goals, and then maintain this column at that level.

A NARROW DEFINITION

Any contact who moves forward from the FA column must be an *active prospect*. Remember, the D.E.I. definition of a prospect is very narrow. In order to move your contact out of the FA column and into one of the columns to the right on the board, you must *verify* that the prospect is in fact playing ball with you by moving through the sales process.

For a field salesperson, that means asking for and receiving a scheduled next appointment, typically before you leave the first meeting.

DO THIS: Ask for the next meeting at the conclusion of the first one.

If the contact is a *real* prospect and is truly playing ball with you, he or she will agree to your request for a second appointment. That means your contact will land in either the 25 percent, 50 percent, or 90 percent category. (We'll discuss these in Chapters 10, 11, and 12.)

Please complete the *Quick Quiz* for Chapter 9 before continuing with the next chapter.

QUICK QUIZ: CHAPTER 9

Please circle your answers.

1. The First Appointment (or FA) column tracks . . .

   a. First appointments you have set but not yet gone out on.
   b. First appointments you have already gone out on.
   c. Friendly answers you receive to questions you pose over the phone.
   d. Instances of frightening aggression you encounter from prospects.

2. The telemarketing equivalent of the first appointment is the initial contact, which occurs when . . .

   a. You have your first "good conversation" with a prospect.
   b. You have your second "good conversation" or "productive call" with a prospect.
   c. You have your third "good conversation" or "productive call" with a prospect.
   d. You leave a persuasive voice mail message.

3. Maintaining a consistent and appropriate level of FAs (or, if you're a telemarketer, initial contacts) is . . .

   a. Optional.
   b. Something that pretty much takes care of itself.
   c. Essential.
   d. Only recommended for salespeople who are inheriting new territories.

Check your answers at the back of this book.

10

The 50 Percent Column

Let's look now at the key prospect category. That's the one that's right in the middle of the board, the 50 percent category. If the prospect reaches this point we have a 50-50 chance of closing the sale. This is the "yes or no" point where the sale could go either way.

This paragraph (that's right, the one you're reading right now) may be the most important one in the entire book. Ready? My experience with literally hundreds of thousands of salespeople leads me to conclude that *those who learn to categorize the 50 percent category correctly, and who maintain the FA column at the proper level, virtually always hit their sales goals.* If you do those two things, you, too, will take control of your own sales process and hit or exceed your sales quota. That's my promise to you.

Taking control is what this system is all about. Mastering the 50 percent column and the FA column really does mean assuming control of your sales process to such a degree that you can accurately predict your own results! (See Chapter 18, which covers forecasting.)

THE PROSPECT MANAGEMENT SYSTEM CATEGORIES

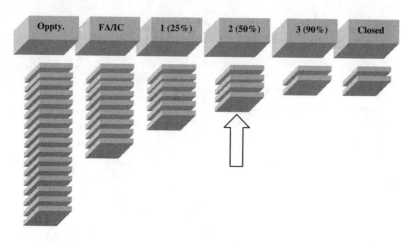

As you read what follows in this chapter, consider the potential benefit to your career of mastering the few simple concepts we'll be covering here. If you would like to join the ranks of those who set high targets for themselves and then hit those targets routinely, the simple classification system that follows will definitely be of interest to you.

SIMPLE, STRICT CRITERIA

Prospects do not reach the 50 percent category because of hunches or subjective whims. What we "feel" about a prospect doesn't matter. In order for us to designate a contact as a 50 percent prospect, certain standards *must* be observed.

Before placing any prospect in this category, be absolutely sure that the following five criteria are met:

1. *You're talking to the right person.* It is *essential* to be in current discussions with the actual decision maker. You aren't investing the time and effort necessary to prepare and deliver a formal quote to someone who will run somewhere else with it or take it to the boss. (Exception: If your

contact has a demonstrated ability to get decisions made in your area of interest, you may consider that contact to be a decision maker.)

2. *The proposal makes sense.* This means that whatever you are proposing fits into what the prospect is looking to do. This relates to our definition of selling.

3. *The budget is right.* You know that the pricing will work. Of course, the final pricing of every element of your proposal may not be settled, but it is absolutely imperative that you discuss the basic pricing framework with your prospect before placing him or her in the 50 percent category.

4. *The timetable is right.* There are two critical timelines that both you and the prospect must understand. These are: the decision date (the point at which a formal choice to work with you or some other vendor must be made) and the implementation date (the point at which a product or service will be used or delivered). These elements are absolutely crucial. If you fail to ask about either of them, then you have not established a workable timetable, no matter what the contact says! Your contact may tell you that decisions will be made "soon" (translation: never) or that delivery or rampup will take place ASAP (translation: never). To appear in the 50 percent column, your prospect must have discussed specific *dates* in each of these areas with you, and those timelines must be within your normal sale cycle.

5. *There is a next step.* You and your prospect agree on when and how you will next discuss where things are going from here. Remember: Without a scheduled next step you don't have a prospect, you have an opportunity.

KEY POINT: For a prospect to show up in the 50 percent category, you must be sure that you are talking to the right person, that the proposal makes sense, that the budget is right, that the timetable is right and matches your average selling cycle, and that you have a next step.

When *all* of the above is true, you can assume that the prospect has a 50 percent chance of closing. If *any* of the above is not true, the contact in question does not belong in the 50 percent category.

> **KEY POINT:** If you sell exclusively over the phone, eligible prospects can, of course, be assigned to the 50 percent category, even though you may never have met them face to face.

A FEW WORDS ON PRICING

For many of the salespeople we train, the discussion of pricing with prospects and contacts can be an emotional subject.

Different salespeople have different approaches to the question of exactly how to discuss pricing issues with their contacts. My own strategy is to throw numbers out and see what happens. It's direct, it's honest, and it's often very entertaining.

When I go out on a sales call, I tell prospects during our first meeting, "Let me tell you what this program is likely to cost you." I name a figure and I watch the reaction that I get, both verbal and nonverbal. By doing this, I am throwing out the ball! Often, when someone says, "Okay, that price is no problem," their facial expressions and physical bearings tell me a very different story. In such a situation, I know I'll have to gather more information about the person's budget, expectations, or past history if I hope to win the business.

As I say, different people take different approaches to this issue. My feeling is that if you bring up price early in the process, instead of waiting for the other person to bring up the issue later in the process, you will, at the very least, know exactly where you stand. What's more, you will have inoculated yourself against future price problems. If you clarify the budget issue during the information-gathering phase (which is much better than finding out about it when you're trying to close!), you're ready to move on to other questions.

REVIEW THE CRITERIA, REMEMBER YOUR SALES CYCLE

Do I really have to know all *that?*

Yes. The 50 percent criteria are extremely important. Be sure to review them closely before you continue with this book. If you do not score 100 percent on the Quick Quiz that concludes this chapter, you are not yet ready to move on to the rest of the material in this book.

A word of warning: Very often, salespeople forget about their own average selling cycles when they are reviewing these criteria. It's probably the easiest of the 50 percent criteria to overlook. Therefore, people often place prospects in the 50 percent category who don't really belong there. This corrupts the system.

Someone who promises to buy six months from now, for instance, should go back into the opportunity column and not forward into 50 percent column. Far too many things can happen over the course of those six months for us to count on that income.

A SIMPLE SALES DIAGNOSTIC STRATEGY

Here, then, is the key point. If you manage the FA and 50 percent columns correctly, you will be successful. If you don't, you will struggle.

After you do a little math, it's fairly easy to figure out how many FAs you need to set each day and how many should be in play at any given point in time. But how can you be absolutely *sure* you're classifying your 50 percent prospects accurately over time? Here's an easy diagnostic strategy you can use.

Review *all* of your 50 percent prospects in this category. For each one, ask yourself the question: How long has this been on my board? Total up the number of weeks for each one of your 50 percent prospects, then divide *that* figure by the total number of prospects in your 50 percent column.

If you're categorizing correctly, you should get a number equal to roughly half of the time you typically need to complete your sales cycle. So, if it takes you, on average, six weeks to close a sale, the average number of weeks on the board for people in this column should be close to three.

You can adapt the same principles to a shorter sales cycle quite easily. Let's say you're selling in a telemarketing environment, and it takes you, on average, six phone contacts to close the sale. Total up the number of calls you have made to all the prospects you've assigned to the 50 percent column. Then divide that figure by the number of prospects in the column. The average you get should be the in the neighborhood of three calls.

WHAT 50 PERCENT REALLY MEANS

When a prospect goes into the 50 percent category, that really means that you either have submitted or are about to submit a certain kind of proposal or recommendation—one that is customized and rock-solid, based on all of the information you've uncovered during your information-gathering step.

In other words, 50 percent prospects should be people who are evaluating a unique proposal from you—one that you honestly believe matches their objectives. In addition to the other criteria we have discussed in this chapter, you should follow this rule for the all-important 50 percent group: *If you have any doubts about whether or not this is the right deal, do not place your prospect in the 50 percent category!*

That, in essence, is the "soft" rule for evaluating 50 percent prospects. Before you move on to the Quick Quiz at the end of this chapter, take one last look at the five "hard" criteria for entry into the 50 percent category. These five yardsticks, when taken together with your own "soft" assessment—your gut feeling about whether or not you've got a proposal that matches what this person does—should guide you in your assignment of contacts to this all-important category.

To determine if your prospect meets the five criteria to become a 50 percent prospect, ask yourself:

1. Is this the right prospect (decision maker or person capable of getting the decision made)?
2. Is this the right deal (makes sense to the other person because it's based on what he or she does)?
3. Is this the right budget (price or price range discussed directly with prospect)?
4. Is this the right timetable (both for making the decision and for implementation)? Does the timetable match your selling cycle?
5. Do I have a next step?

Please complete the *Quick Quiz* for Chapter 10 before continuing with the next chapter.

QUICK QUIZ: CHAPTER 10

Please circle your answers.

1. Which of the following elements are required for classification as a 50 percent prospect? (Circle all that apply.)

   a. Signed contract in hand
   b. Next step established
   c. Verbal agreement to buy established

    d. Prospect has toured your facility

    e. Right timetable established

    f. Travel aspects of prospect's CEO faxed to all team members

    g. Right budget established

    h. Proposal makes sense to you and to prospect

    i. Right specifications for final implementation approved in writing by representative of prospect company

    j. Right person (decision maker or someone who can get decision made) is in discussion with you

2. To be classified as a 50 percent prospect, it is necessary to have met in person with your contact.

    a. True

    b. False

3. A contact has met with you a number of times and appears extremely interested in what you have to sell. This contact will not, however, discuss dates or dollar figures with you. Should you classify this person as a 50 percent prospect? (Select the answer that is correct and provides the proper reasoning for your response.)

    a. Yes, because you have a very strong "gut feeling" that the sale has a 50 percent chance of closing.

    b. Yes, because you are absolutely certain that you are dealing with the correct decision maker.

    c. No, because you have met with this prospect more than once.

    d. No, because prospects that still will not discuss budget frameworks or delivery dates cannot be assigned to the 50 percent category.

Check your answers at the back of this book.

11

The 90 Percent Column

O_{ur} 90 percent category represents a verbal agreement to do business together. People in this group meet all of our criteria for the 90 percent category and they have said clearly and directly to us something such as, "We are going to use what you have to offer. We want to get started September 1."

THE PROSPECT MANAGEMENT SYSTEM CATEGORIES

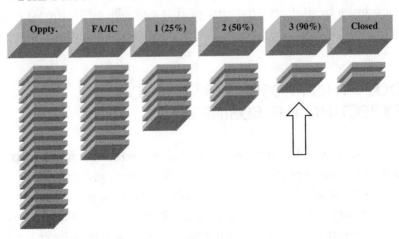

We categorize people in this group as 90 percent, rather than 100 percent or closed because there is still a chance for the deal to fall through, even though it might be the right person saying yes. Prospects in this category are also described as "C.O.D.," which stands for "contract on desk."

> **KEY POINT:** The next step criteria still applies here. We have to have an established date and time to complete the formalities. After everything is signed, the prospect can be moved to the closed category.

ARE YOU WILLING TO BET YOUR PAYCHECK?

Sometimes salespeople are a little too eager to place prospects in the 90 percent category. They put people in this grouping whom they believe to be likely to close. That is *not* the same as meeting all of the 50 percent criteria *and* offering a verbal agreement to do business together.

In order to remind our own salespeople of the distinction, I sometimes ask, "Are you willing to bet your paycheck on this deal?" If the answer is no—or if the answer includes even a moment's hesitation—the prospect is not placed in the 90 percent column.

DOES THIS PROSPECT KNOW YOU ARE EXPECTING THE BUSINESS?

If you have classified someone at 90 percent who does not *know* you are expecting to close the deal, there is a problem!

Ask yourself: Do I have any doubt on this score? Is there any uncertainty whatsoever regarding whether or not the person I am speaking with is *actually aware* of the fact that I expect to close this deal? If you hold any such doubt, simply hold the prospect back in the 50 percent column until you have had a conversation like the following with your prospect.

> **You** "You know, when I come back tomorrow with our revised proposal, I'm going to assume that we can set up dates and get started."
>
> **Prospect:** "Yeah, that sounds good."

Here is another way it could sound. As you leave the prospect's office after your second or third "good meeting," you might initiate a dialogue that sounds something like this.

> **You:** "Gee, I have to tell you, I'm really happy about the way this seems to be going. How do you feel about it?"
>
> **Prospect:** "I have to say, I feel pretty good about it, too. Things seem to be moving forward. I like what I'm seeing."
>
> **You:** "That's great to hear. Listen, just between you and me, where do you think this is going? What do you think is going to happen here over the next (week, ten days, quarter)?"
>
> **Prospect:** "To tell you the truth, I think we are looking pretty good. I think we are going to end up doing business together."

KEY POINT: If you do not get this kind of response from your prospect, you do not have a verbal agreement to do business, and you are not looking at a 90 percent situation.

It should go without saying, of course, that any prospect whom you categorize as a 90 percent prospect after such a discussion must already be familiar with the pricing, scheduling, and other particulars of the proposal you have assembled, *and* in a position to give you a positive response on that proposal.

Please complete the *Quick Quiz* for Chapter 11 before continuing with the next chapter.

QUICK QUIZ: CHAPTER 11

Please circle your answers.

1. Prospects in the 90 percent category do not need to meet all of the criteria for 50 percent prospects.

   a. True
   b. False

2. Prospects in the 90 percent category are also described as . . . .

   a. Cash on delivery.
   b. Committed on desperation.
   c. Contract on desk.
   d. Close or deliver.

3. If you are not willing to bet your paycheck that a given deal will close, you should . . .

   a. Arrange for a smaller paycheck.
   b. Still categorize the lead as 90 percent.
   c. Recategorize the contact into a column to the left of 90 percent on the Prospect Board.
   d. Move the prospect into the closed category.

Check your answers at the back of this book.

12

The 25 Percent Column

Before we reach the all-important 50 percent category, we find a group for slightly less-qualified prospects. This is the 25 percent category—the least-advanced of the three active prospect columns. This group is placed immediately before the 50 percent group on the board.

THE PROSPECT MANAGEMENT SYSTEM CATEGORIES

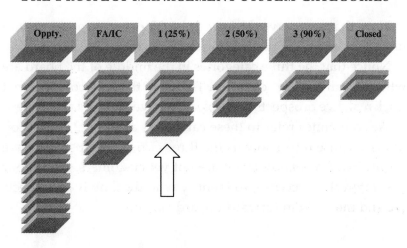

This column is best considered the not-quite-eligible-for-50-percent category. The 25 percent column is for prospects who are past the first appointment stage and committed to a next step, but do not meet all of the 50 percent criteria.

KEY POINT: The 25 percent column is for people who are past the first appointment stage and are, in fact, playing ball with you, but, for whatever reason, do not meet all of the criteria for the 50 percent column.

The only mandatory element for being a 25 percent prospect is having met with the salesperson and scheduled a next step.

Our objective for these prospects is simply to get them to meet all of the 50 percent category criteria.

DO THIS: Make it your goal to move prospects in the 25 percent category forward so that they meet all the requirements for the 50 percent category.

THE THREE ACTIVE PROSPECT CATEGORIES

Now that you have reviewed the 25 percent category, you have explored all of the categories on the board.

Notice that the three categories in the middle of the board are what we call "active" columns. These are the only columns that track real, live prospects—people who have given us a next step.

We sometimes refer to these categories as the 1, 2, and 3 columns because they show us the three critical groups who have *demonstrated commitment* but are not yet customers. It is in our best interests, of course, to identify who these active prospects are and move them forward toward closure.

THE PROSPECT MANAGEMENT SYSTEM CATEGORIES

Once again: *Our goal is always to focus on active prospects whenever we can and move those active contacts through the process.* That is to say, we want to turn 25 percent prospects into 50 percent prospects, 50 percent prospects into 90 percent prospects, and 90 percent prospect into customers.

Please complete the *Quick Quiz* for Chapter 12 before continuing with the next chapter.

QUICK QUIZ: CHAPTER 12

Please circle your answers.

1. The 25 percent column is for people who . . .

   a. Are past the first appointment stage and are, in fact, playing ball with you, but for some reason do not meet all of the criteria for the 50 percent column.
   b. Have not yet spoken to you.
   c. Have paid 25 percent of the amount of money they owe your company.
   d. Will not agree to do business with you.

2. The three categories in the middle of the prospect board are called "active" columns because . . .

   a. They all require action from the salesperson and sales manager working as a team.
   b. They are the only columns that track real, live prospects—people who have actually given us a next step.
   c. They have actively told us that they have no interest in buying from us.
   d. They are designed for people who have active, outgoing personalities.

3. Our goal with 25 percent prospects is to . . .

   a. Determine their needs.
   b. Move them into the first appointment column.
   c. Move them into the 50 percent column.
   d. Find their pain.

Check your answers at the back of this book.

13

Reinforcing the Categories

You have now identified and reviewed the six different categories:

1. Fallbacks (also known as opportunities)
2. First appointments (also known as initial contacts if you are selling within a telemarketing environment)
3. 25 percent
4. 50 percent
5. 90 percent
6. Closed

On the following pages, you will find a short summary of all six of these categories and their criteria. You may want to photocopy this summary for your own personal use as you become more familiar with the system.

Keep the summary sheets near your work area, where you can refer to them easily.

QUICK REVIEW: THE PROSPECT MANAGEMENT SYSTEM CATEGORIES

Fallbacks/opportunities. These are people with whom you have not yet made initial contact and are not yet prospects. These are candidates, suspects, leads, or referrals—people we want to do business with, but with whom we do not yet have a real relationship.

First appointments/initial contacts. *For people who sell face to face:* These are decisions makers with whom we have scheduled an appointment for a specific date and time. *For telemarketers:* These are decision makers with whom we have had at least two good conversations. (One good discussion is *not* enough to move into this column.)

25 percent. *This is the first active prospect column.* This category is for people who are in the process with us—and have committed to a next step—but do not meet all of the criteria for a 50 percent prospect.

50 percent. *This is the second active prospect column.* This category is for situations where we are talking to the right person about a proposal that makes sense; we are also talking specifically about budgets and pricing; we have a timeline that matches up with our average sales cycle; and we have a next step with this person. The 50 percent column is the key column. If you classify people in this group correctly, the system will work well for you.

90 percent. *This is the third active prospect column.* This category is for people who have given us a verbal agreement to buy. This category is also known as the "contract on desk" category. Nine out of ten prospects in this category should turn into business for you. If you are not willing to bet your paycheck on the deal, do not place the prospect in this column.

Closed. This is for customers. This category represents a formal commitment to use what your organization offers. It may reflect, for instance, the receipt of a signed contract. People in this column, of course, may also represent future business for us.

TIME AND THE SELLING CYCLE

Look at the graph to see how time affects the selling cycle. Notice again how most prospects drop out and *fail* to move from zero to 100 percent in the system.

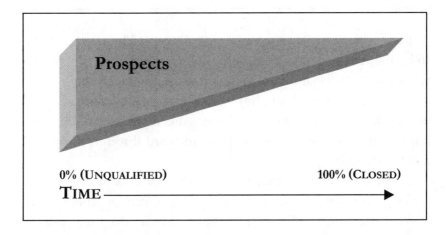

This is the visual representation of a principle with which you should be quite familiar with by now: There is *no such thing* as closing every sale. We can expect some prospects to drop out of the process over time.

KEY POINT: Time affects the selling cycle.

Now compare that pattern to the formation that you have been looking at in Chapters 7 through 12.

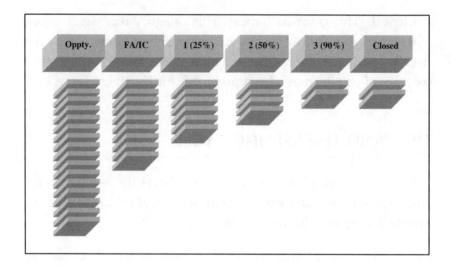

This formation—also quite familiar by now, I hope—happens to be the ideal board formation. This general shape is actually what you want your board to look like on any given day.

Notice that this ideal shape, too, tails off. Of course, you already know why. The categories get shorter as you move from left to right because as people move forward through the cycle, most of them drop off.

So, we've come full circle now. We can understand the whole process. We can see clearly that not all of our prospects will make it from start to finish, and that any individual rejection is part of a natural process we are guiding and supporting. We are not surprised to hear the word *no* because we already know that people are going to drop off along the way!

KEY POINT: Most contacts drop out of the Prospect Management System. That's why we have to make sure the FA column is well stocked at all times.

Because we know that the system requires us to replace *more* than one prospect for every sale we make, we can identify exactly how many prospects need to go back into the system after each sale. We can also be prepared to keep a close watch on our first appointment/initial contact column, making sure that it is always our longest column.

WHAT IS HAPPENING IN YOUR PROSPECT BASE?

Using this system, we can visualize exactly what is happening with all of our prospects at any given point in time. We can instantly see how what we are doing matches up with that ideal formation.

Every time we look at our prospects in the various categories, we must remind ourselves how important that first appointment/initial contact column is. That column is what makes everything else happen. In fact, if we were to spend a week or two—or even longer!—focusing *only* on prospects in the 25 percent, 50 percent, and 90 percent columns, without initiating any initial contacts whatsoever, what would happen?

I hope that, by now, the answer to that question is automatic for you. We would find ourselves playing catch-up, because even though we are moving prospects forward into the closed category, we are not identifying new people in the initial contact category. These are people who are *going to become our next* 25 percent, 50 percent, and 90 percent prospects.

Please complete the *Quick Quiz* for Chapter 13 before continuing with the next chapter.

QUICK QUIZ: CHAPTER 13

Please circle your answers.

1. Which column of the system is for people who have given you a verbal agreement to do business and have a contract on their desk?

   a. Opportunities/fallbacks
   b. First appointment/initial contact
   c. 1 (25 percent)
   d. 2 (50 percent)
   e. 3 (90 percent)
   f. Closed

2. Which column is for situations where you are: talking to the right person about a proposal that makes sense; discussing specific budgets and timetables with that person; and certain about the next step?

   a. Opportunities/fallbacks
   b. First appointment/initial contact
   c. 1 (25 percent)
   d. 2 (50 percent)
   e. 3 (90 percent)
   f. Closed

3. Which column is for someone with whom you have had one good conversation but have not established a next step?

   a. Opportunities/fallbacks
   b. First appointment/initial contact
   c. 1 (25 percent)
   d. 2 (50 percent)
   e. 3 (90 percent)
   f. Closed

4. Which column is for someone with whom you have had two good conversations but have not established a next step?

   a. Opportunities/fallbacks
   b. First appointment/initial contact
   c. 1 (25 percent)
   d. 2 (50 percent)
   e. 3 (90 percent)
   f. Closed

5. Which column is for prospects who are in discussion with you and have set up a next step but do not fall into the could-go-either-way category because they are missing one or more of the criteria for that column?

   a. Opportunities/fallbacks
   b. First appointment/initial contact
   c. 1 (25 percent)
   d. 2 (50 percent)
   e. 3 (90 percent)
   f. Closed

6. Someone you call for the first time tells you that he is extremely unhappy with the current supplier, but will not commit to a date and time to talk to you about your product or service. How should this person be classified?

   a. Opportunities/fallbacks
   b. First appointment/initial contact
   c. 1 (25 percent)
   d. 2 (50 percent)
   e. 3 (90 percent)
   f. Closed

Check your answers at the back of this book.

14

Tracking Changes in Your Board over Time

Your Prospect Board must be date driven, and must be evaluated regularly.

Weekly reevaluation of *everything* on your Prospect Board is mandatory if you want this system to work for you.

> **DO THIS:** Date all your entries and check the dates regularly. Review and reclassify the entries on your Prospect Board at least once a week.

The date of the scheduled first appointment (or, in the case of an initial contact, the dates of the first and second "good calls") should be noted on all cards and all entries except opportunities. These dates must be constantly compared to your average selling cycle. If the entries are too old, drop them back to the opportunities column.

YOUR SELLING CYCLE—ANALYZED VIA THE PROSPECT MANAGEMENT SYSTEM

Take a few minutes to determine how much time an average sale will spend *in each of the six categories*. Remember, these numbers should reflect your own unique selling environment.

Here's an example of what you might come up with.

- To move from opportunities to first appointment: one week.
- To move from first appointment to 25 percent: three days
- To move from 25 percent to 50 percent: two weeks
- To move from 50 percent to 90 percent: one week
- To move from 90 percent to close: one week

If these were your numbers, verified through actual experience, you would know for certain that your own selling cycle—first appointment to close—was approximately five and a half weeks. You would know that it typically took you a week to get someone out of the opportunities column. You would know that you spent most of your time moving prospects from 25 percent to 50 percent.

Significant deviations from that pattern would start to set off warning signals. If you saw such variations, you would want to say to yourself: "Something's wrong here! What can I do differently?"

BOARD FORMATIONS

We're going to take some time now to look at common board formations that *deviate* from the ideal—and strategize what you should do about them.

Let's look closely now at the three active categories of the ideal formation.

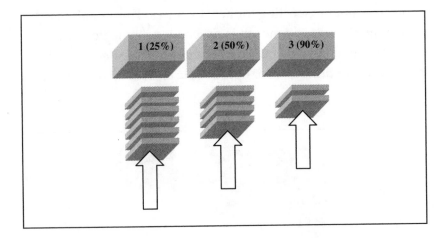

As we have seen, this is an excellent formation for any salesperson prospecting proactively for new business. If we maintain this formation, we will always have a constant stream of income. Unfortunately, it's not always easy to post the ideal formation. In fact, most of the salespeople we train get distracted from doing so, for any number of reasons. The hard truth is, it takes effort and constant self-correction to maintain the right formation.

Suppose our board looked like this one.

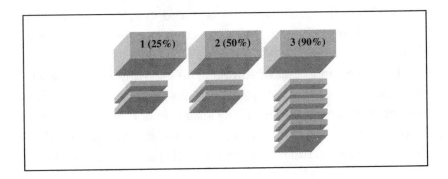

In the short term, this formation is great because the salesperson is making numerous sales and, we hope, lots of money! However, in the long term, this salesperson will have nothing because he or she is not prospecting for new business. This month may be a good month but next month is probably going to be terrible.

That formation shows what happens when someone neglects to prospect continuously for new people and set up first appointments.

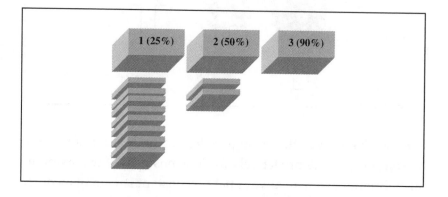

This formation could indicate the results of a new salesperson who is just getting started. There has been a lot of solid prospecting, as reflected in the 25 percent column. But there is nothing closing immediately. This formation could also belong to someone who has made a lot of sales and then suddenly found themselves with nothing. This person is forced to make a lot of calls over a week or so to begin the prospecting step with a lot of new people.

If the situation is that of someone just starting out, the strategy would be to work with senior management to ensure that presentations are on target. If the situation is that of an experienced rep trying to make up for lost time, the solution is, alas, simply to prospect full time until the crisis passes, and then keep up a disciplined, intelligent daily prospecting effort so that the same problem doesn't arise again.

It is unfortunate but true that the formation shown at left *usually* belongs to someone who has simply stopped prospecting for awhile and is moving back toward the ideal formation. This is, as a general rule, a fairly painful period of time.

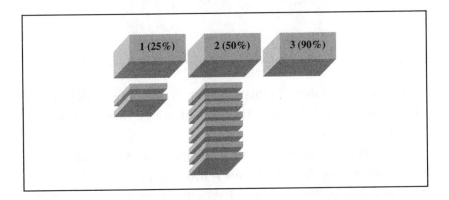

In the above case, I would be curious to know why more prospects have not progressed from the 50 percent column to the 90 percent column. Wouldn't you?

This is the "pending proposal formation." Everything is pending a decision. Nothing is actually happening.

If you find that little or nothing is moving forward from 50 percent to 90 percent over an extended period of time, you should sit down with your manager and work through the proposals you've been developing.

Are they all based on what makes sense to the prospects? Are you really learning what makes sense to the prospect in the first place? Have you asked for the business by saying, "Makes sense to me. What do you think?"

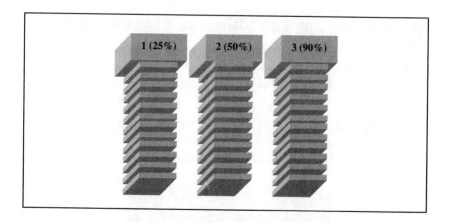

Here's my question: Is this salesperson being realistic? I think the answer is probably no. There wouldn't be time to complete all of these sales!

This formation is typical for someone who is not yet categorizing accurately or who is not removing prospects that have dropped out of the process. Remember, as prospects move through the process, *most of them fall out!*

This formation typically shows up among salespeople who are not yet conducting effective *weekly* reviews of their Prospect Boards. Again: To track the activities, the system needs constant updating.

Please complete the *Quick Quiz* for Chapter 14 before continuing with the next chapter.

QUICK QUIZ: CHAPTER 14

Please circle your answers.

1. Weekly reevaluation of *everything* on your prospect board is . . .

   a. Recommended.
   b. Prohibitively time-consuming.
   c. Traumatic.
   d. Mandatory.

2. In order for a prospect to appear in the 25 percent, 50 percent or 90 percent column, there *must* be a . . .

   a. Legally binding commitment to work exclusively with your company.
   b. Date for the next appointment or step. For instance: Call Monday, January 1, for the decision.
   c. Committee formed to investigate whether criteria for inclusion on your board of directors has been circulated throughout the company.
   d. "Gut feeling" that the sale has a good chance of closing.

3. Deviations from the amount of time it typically takes you to move from one step to another on the Prospect Board should . . .

   a. Not concern you at all because every sale is unique.
   b. Make you wonder "What's wrong here?"
   c. Encourage you because the longer your sale takes, the more money it is likely to be worth and the likelier it is to close.
   d. Motivate you to write a letter to the features editor of your local newspaper.

Check your answers at the back of this book.

15

Common Questions about the Prospect Management System

How do I apply the system to my base of existing business?

It may take some practice to categorize new potential business within existing accounts. Many salespeople overestimate their chances for doing new business with customers, or get stuck because they are used to applying a system of their own.

> **DO THIS:** Be realistic about the status of discussions with current customers.

Adapt the same criteria to classify possibilities for doing business with customers that you use with new accounts. Be just as vigilant when identifying the relevance, criteria, and commitments of your present contacts as you would with a prospect you just developed. Fight any temptation to inflate the status of your discussions with current customers.

Here, as elsewhere, you must be honest with yourself and feed good information in, or the system will be worthless to you.

Are all of my unqualified leads supposed to go in the opportunities column?

Probably not. Your opportunities column could conceivably be many times the length the column space seen in the illustrations in this book. Usually, though, we find that salespeople are most comfortable working with about ten opportunities at any given time.

I've got a prospect that doesn't seem to fall into any of the categories you've described! What should I do?

These situations won't come up very often. Occasionally, though, you will run into an organization that doesn't seem to match up with anything we've talked about—a situation where there are dual decision makers, perhaps. Maybe one of them is ecstatic about what you have to offer and the other doesn't ever want to talk to you. Put the exception aside and deal with it individually. Don't use it as an excuse not to keep the rest of the information up to date.

If you and your manager disagree about the placement of a contact within the Prospect Management System, follow your supervisor's lead and classify the contact as conservatively as possible.

Let the disagreement serve as a challenge to you! Find a way to prove beyond a shadow of a doubt to your manager—and to yourself!—that the contact does in fact belong in a higher category.

What else do I need to know about an entry into the system besides the name of my contacts and the name of the organization?

You need to specify what's going to happen next—and when! Any entry that leaves the opportunities category must be updated regularly. Save all your entries and check all the dates at least weekly, preferably as part of a team meeting! (See Chapter 16.) Remember, *if you are not reviewing and, where appropriate, reclassifying all your prospects at least once a week, you will not get the benefit from the system that you should.*

The Prospect Board is part of a dynamic system. A prospect that stays in the same place for any significant length of time probably reflects a problem somewhere in your selling process. For example, if you notice after two or three weeks that a card hasn't moved anywhere, you should either put it back in the opportunities column or take it out of the system all together.

I cannot emphasize the point enough: If you can't answer the question "What's happening next with this person?" then you are not dealing with an active prospect. This person may belong in the opportunities category or may need to be removed from the board altogether.

PART THREE

Getting Up and Running

16

The Art of the Board Review

Where I work, we are strong advocates of weekly board review sessions.

This is simply a sales meeting that takes place on a regular basis (every Monday, for instance) in which all the sales reps on a given team answer questions from a meeting leader about *everything* that appears on the board. In other words, each salesperson is *accountable* for the placement of each contact on the board. Specifically, each salesperson must be willing to justify:

- How long a contact has been on the board
- Whether or not a contact has been evaluated correctly
- What the scheduled next step with the prospect is
- What the team's next step should be

Conducting an effective board review on a weekly basis can transform your company's culture and dramatically improve your overall sales performance.

Board reviews (which can be led either by a manager or by one of the senior salespeople on the team) are always eye-opening experiences. We recommend that the sales reps keep track of their own contacts on a personal Prospect Board, and that the team use a larger magnetic board to track the activity of the group as a whole. If your organization decides to follow this approach, you will find, as we and countless other companies have, that bringing the two groupings of prospects into harmony once a week is an essential routine for effective selling.

HOW THE MEETING IS STRUCTURED

The structure of a board review meeting is simple. The leader of the meeting calls on each team member and reviews all the active prospects (25 percent, 50 percent, and 90 percent) that individual has placed on his or her board over the course of the previous week. At the same time, the leader adjusts the larger "team board" to match the final assessment of each contact.

QUESTIONS DRIVE THE MEETING

Make no mistake. The board review meeting is an opportunity to *ask tough questions* about the prospects on a salesperson's board. If you are leading the meeting, you must take advantage of that opportunity. If you are taking part in the meeting, you should learn to accept—gratefully!—the chance to look more realistically at your prospect classifications each week.

KEY POINT: For most of us, selling means losing some of our objectivity. We want to believe the best about each new selling situation. Allowing other people to critique our Prospect Board offers us an essential reality check.

It's true: *If the questions aren't tough, the board review is unlikely to be effective.* When, on the other hand, the meeting leader isn't afraid to challenge the group's classifications, there is a far lower chance of prospects being miscategorized.

What follows are some of the most effective questioning categories and specific questions we have developed in the 15 years that have passed since we introduced the Prospect Management System. If it's your job to lead the meeting, don't ask the following questions aggressively or obnoxiously—but do ask them, and don't accept unconvincing responses!

By making a habit of posing key questions about people in the active prospect categories, you will encourage other team members to find out the answers to these questions *before they walk into the weekly board review meeting.*

Prospect Status Questions

- When did you first meet with this prospect? *(Very important because the system is date-driven! Be sure the date of the first meeting is recorded on the board.)*
- When are you going back? *(Very important because the system requires a next step with a specific date and time. If there is no specific date and time, recategorize!)*
- Did you ask for a second appointment at the conclusion of the first meeting—while you were on site? If not, why not?
- How much is this worth?

Contact Questions

- Who's your contact? What is his or her title?
- Is this the final decision maker?
- How long has he or she been with the organization?
- How did he or she get the job?
- Who is this person's boss?
- How long has he or she been reporting to his or her boss?
- Why are you meeting with him or her?
- What would he or she have done if you hadn't called and asked for an appointment?

Company Questions

- What does the company do? (*If you don't know, how can you expect to help them do what they do better?*)
- How long has the company been in business?
- What is the company doing now to train its salespeople, update its computer systems, keep track of its widgets, etc.?
- Who are the company's customers?
- What are the company's future plans?
- What is your plan when you go back? How did you determine that that was the right plan?

Alliance Questions

- Who else has this company looked at in the past?
- Why didn't those solutions make sense?
- Who else is this company looking at now?
- Why are they looking at them?

Activity Questions

- What were your ratios last week? *(Did you track them? Do you know what you are attempting to improve this week?)*
- Specifically, how many dials did you make?
- How many people did you get through to?
- How many people do you have to speak to in order to get an appointment?
- How many appointments do you need to hit your goals?

Please complete the *Quick Quiz* for Chapter 16 before continuing with the next chapter.

QUICK QUIZ: CHAPTER 16

Please circle your answers.

1. Which set of numbers represents the *active* prospects that a salesperson should place on his or her board?

   a. 25, 50, 95
   b. 25, 50, 90
   c. 30, 60, 90

2. What are some examples of effective questions to ask to best determine the status of a prospect?

   a. When are you going back?
   b. When did you first meet with the prospect?
   c. How much is this deal worth?
   d. All of the above.

3. During a sales meeting, a salesperson must be willing to justify . . .

   a. That he or she is only meeting with Fortune 100 firms.
   b. That a prospect is working exclusively with his or her company.
   c. What the scheduled next step with any given prospect should be.

Check your answers at the back of this book.

17

Using Team Selling to Rescue Lost Sales

Often, our questions during the board review meeting push contacts back from one of the active categories into a category one or more levels lower. Perhaps the team concludes that a contact that had been categorized as 90 percent should really go into 25 percent. Perhaps a contact that had originally gone into 25 percent drops back to the opportunities column.

What can you do to "rescue" these prospects and move them forward toward the closed category?

I've noticed that the most successful sales reps learn when and how to bring management in for help when prospects drop back. These reps realize that they cannot always close a deal solo; wisely, they turn to their higher-ups for assistance. The board review meeting is an excellent time to strategize this kind of help.

Let's say an experienced sales representative is at the proposal stage with a prospect but is no longer certain about the timetable, pricing, person, or plan. The prospect has to drop back from 50 percent, where it had been placed, to 25 percent.

At this point, why not call in the sales manager?

Here's one way it can work. The sales manager might call this prospect and say something along the following lines: "I just wanted to call and say hello. I'm Frank Randolph, the sales manager at ABC. I understand from speaking with my rep, Malvina Perez, that it looks like we'll be doing business together."

What's likely to happen? If the prospect says, "Yes, that's right," and then talks about the budget and the timeline, then Frank knows that this prospect does in fact deserve to be put back at the 50 percent level.

If, on the other hand, Frank hears, "What? Gee, I'm not so sure about that." He can ask, "Oh, what seems to be the issue?"

At our company, the sales manager deals with any negative issues that arise by offering examples of how we have helped other customers in similar situations.

MANAGER'S RESOURCE: Work with your team to develop and practice at least ten compelling success stories. Each should emphasize a slightly different benefit of working with your company.

Bringing in the sales manager (or the head of the company or any other bigwig) has a remarkable way of letting a sales rep know exactly where he or she stands with a prospect. Sometimes, the team finds that there is no possibility of working together in the short term; sometimes it uncovers new vistas of opportunity. The only real crime lies in *not trying* to move the sale forward by bringing someone else into the picture.

When we use this strategy, I often close the call by saying to our prospect, "I will work with Malvina Perez to deal with the concern you've raised. You can be assured we will work together to make sure you are comfortable in this area."

Then what happens? Well, let's say the rep then meets with his or her contact and *doesn't* get the deal. The sales manager can then make a second call.

Can you guess what that call's going to focus on? It's certainly *not* going to accuse the prospect of misleading the rep! Instead, it's going to showcase the team's willingness to take responsibility for the situation. It might sound like this: "I was talking to Malvina Perez today, and she mentioned that we are not going to be doing business together after all. Did we do something wrong?"

Once the manager or other team member has posed this question and listened to the response, he or she should ask the person directly, but without aggression or self-pity, *why* there is no deal. The explanation you receive will almost always begin with the words, "The thing is . . . ." That's a good sign!

The approach I'm outlining represents one of the most underrated reclamation strategies in the industry. It leaves the door open for a future relationship and usually gives you all the information you need to approach the prospect later on.

Very often, the follow-up call built around "What did we do wrong?" will get you another appointment and a chance to salvage *this* sale. When this happens (and it will if you make a habit of the ideas I'm discussing), the sales manager or other colleague can simply close the call by saying, "Let's get together with Malvina so we can talk face to face about how we can work together to solve the issues you've raised in such-and-such an area. How about Wednesday at 1:00 PM at your office?"

I think you'll be amazed at how often these ideas will result in major sales for your team—from prospects that appeared to be lost!

Please complete the *Quick Quiz* for Chapter 17 before continuing to the next chapter.

QUICK QUIZ: CHAPTER 17

Please circle your answers.

1. Of the following options, which is the best way for a manager to close a call with a prospect?

   a. "I'll have Malvina give you a call sometime next week."
   b. "Let's get together with Malvina so we can work together to solve this issue. Give me a date and time when we can stop by next week."
   c. "Let's get together with Malvina so we can review how we can work together to solve this issue. How's next Tuesday at 3 PM at your office?"

2. Why is it important to bring a manager in to help rescue a lost sale?

   a. Your manager can always be expected to close the sale over the phone.
   b. Your manager can ask the prospect questions to uncover additional information.
   c. Your manager probably has direct personal knowledge of the prospect's buying habits.

3. One good way for the team to deal with negative issues that arise with prospects is . . .

   a. Explaining your company's products and services in detail.
   b. Asking where you went wrong, listening to the answer, and following up with examples of how your company has helped other customers in similar situations.
   c. Inviting a prospect to a fancy lunch.

Check your answers at the back of this book.

18

Forecasting

The Prospect Management System is a sales tool that has been implemented successfully in virtually every industry. Over the years, we've learned that it is just about perfect as a diagnostic tool—*if* you classify correctly and build your daily to-do list around the right activities. In fact, many of the salespeople we train use the program as their primary time management tool. They focus first on developing new prospects for the FA column, then on closing activities, then on 50 percent prospects, then on 25 percent prospects, and so forth, allotting a certain portion of every day to the relevant columns.

One principle has stood the test of time: The more accurate the information you feed into the Prospect Management System, the more accurate the information you get from it will be.

If you overstate the likelihood of a particular lead turning into dollars, you'll only be fooling yourself. Believe me when I tell you that it won't take you long to find out that the information you fed into the system wasn't realistic! If you set up a board and fill it with prospects who are not willing to talk seriously about doing business with you, you will be in for a very rude awakening. If you set a daily prospecting target and then don't make any effort to hit it, you should not be surprised when you fail to hit quota.

ANTICIPATING REVENUE

All of which brings us to the question of how to use the system to anticipate future revenue.

What do the next weeks or months hold for you in terms of income? The answer is probably easier to learn than you think. If you're interested in finding out how to develop accurate estimates of the income you're likely to receive from the prospects you're currently tracking on the board, read on.

Assign a dollar value to each of the cards in your 25 percent, 50 percent, or 90 percent columns. Add up all the figures in the 25 percent column, then multiply to determine 25 percent of that figure. Add up all the figures in the 50 percent column, then multiply to determine 50 percent of that figure. Add up all the figures in the 90 percent column, then multiply to determine 90 percent of that figure.

Add all three of your totals together and you'll have a pretty good idea of what the revenue generated by your total current prospect base will be.

This method is simple and extremely accurate—*as long as* you classify your contacts correctly and do not try to project beyond your typical selling cycle. (In other words, if your selling cycle is eight weeks, the only truly realistic revenue estimate you can make will be for eight weeks into the future. Everything beyond that will be based on hunches, not on the decisions and feedback you get from active prospects.)

Please complete the *Quick Quiz* for Chapter 18 before continuing with the next chapter.

QUICK QUIZ: CHAPTER 18

Please circle your answers.

1. Find the best ending to this sentence: The more accurate the information you feed into the Prospect Management System . . .

   a. The more accurate the information you get from the system will be.
   b. The more insecure you are likely to become.
   c. The less revenue you are likely to generate.
   d. None of the above.

2. The revenue forecasting strategy discussed in this chapter is accurate as long as you . . .

   a. Compute totals for only the 90 percent category.
   b. Compute totals for only the 50 percent category.
   c. Compute totals for only the 25 percent category.
   d. Classify contacts in all the categories correctly and avoid trying to forecast beyond your current selling cycle.

Check your answers at the back of this book.

19

Case Study: Increasing Revenue with the Prospect Management System

From the Winter 2000/2001 issue of *The Executive Sales Briefing*

Executive Summary. A Canadian company tracks prospects using quantifiable categories. The result: dramatic sales increases that justify new hires within its sales channel. By tracking and categorizing prospects effectively, *the team boosted appointments by 670 percent!*

Clearnet, Inc., is a major Canadian provider of digital wireless communications services with a dealer-based distribution channel. Recently, the company undertook an innovative training program for its dealers. For some time, Clearnet had been attempting to expand the performance of its dealer network, which consists primarily of small businesses. Clearnet's efforts to forecast its income through the dealer channel network had been unsuccessful. No system was in place for tracking or managing sales activity.

Clearnet knew that its dealer principals—the owners or managers of the dealerships—tended to be the top salespeople in their respective areas. The question was how to get *other* salespeople to contribute at higher levels. Many dealer principals reported that they had no time to support and manage the activity of their existing sales teams. In fact, they reported that they were having trouble focusing on their own clients!

How does one go about expanding the sales channel in such a situation? Hiring more salespeople when the existing representatives were not meeting expectations (and when the dealer principals did not have the tools to manage the sales teams effectively) didn't seem to make much sense. Clearnet believed that by using an activity-based forecasting tool to manage the daily activity of salespeople on an ongoing basis, the dealerships could post large enough revenue increases to support the acquisition of sales managers—and new salespeople.

The plan. Clearnet decided to train a pilot group of six "coachable" and "growth-oriented" dealer principals to use the Prospect Management System, a sales relationship management tool. The Prospect Management System uses a very narrow definition to answer the question "Who is a prospect?" (The answer: Someone who has actively committed to a clear next step to discuss establishing a business relationship.) The system tracks quantifiable sales activity and commitment among prospects by means of six categories, each with clear criteria. It holds salespeople accountable for the development of new prospects on a daily basis.

D.E.I. Management Group launched an eight-week program consisting of an in-person Prospect Management training session in week one, six weeks of conference calls to all participants at each dealer, and a final in-person session used to reinforce key concepts.

Trainer Tim O'Brien's responsibility was to manage the prospecting activity of all six dealer principals and all 25 of their representatives. His aim was to do this in such a way as to increase effectiveness—and sales.

Measurement. At the beginning of the first session, Clearnet and D.E.I. conducted a prospect audit of the six dealers and derived figures for total appointments and total load value. (In Clearnet terms, *load value* is a yardstick for sales revenue.) These numbers would serve as a benchmark for comparison at the end of the eight-week program. Initially, there were 40 total appointments and the total load value was 16.8.

Results. The values in each of the two categories increased steadily, week by week, as the training progressed. By the end of the eight-week program, total appointments had risen to 268, a 670 percent increase! Total load value had increased to 152.2, a 910 percent jump. The results were so impressive that all participants insisted that they would continue managing their prospects using the Prospect Management System.

Conclusion. As a result of the training, Clearnet decided to make a friendly suggestion to the dealer principals who took part in the program: Create a sales manager's role within your dealership to oversee compliance with the Prospect Management System—and you'll make more money!

All six of the dealer principals followed Clearnet's suggestion, concluding that the additional revenue associated with using the Prospect Management System would more than offset the expense of creating the new position.

The bottom line. Sales increased because dealer principals used the Prospect Management System to manage sales activity in a systematic manner and hold salespeople accountable for daily prospecting activity. Working as a team, D.E.I. and Clearnet made believers of the dealer principals and their sales representatives, and gave Clearnet and its dealers a significant competitive edge.

(Note: In 2001, Clearnet became part of Telus Mobility.)

20

Ten Principles for
Sales Success

Some years ago, I challenged myself to identify ten reliable rules for success in sales—principles that would hold true across all industries, and in any economic climate.

Here's what I came up with. I have shared the following list with countless salespeople over the years, and it has always elicited a positive response. Many of the people we train have asked for printed copies of the list, which leads me to believe that a written summary as we close this book may be helpful to you.

1. Always set the next appointment during the first meeting. (This accelerates your sales cycle.)
2. Always verify your information. (The easiest way to do this is with an outline or preliminary proposal that allows the prospect to give you verbatim feedback before you make a formal recommendation.)
3. Escalate the sale. (Bring in a manager or other team member.)
4. Always find out what they really do. (Don't assume you already know what they really do; don't assume that this customer is identical to the last one you sold to. Ask "do-based" questions.)

5. Plan two weeks in advance. (Know what you expect to make happen over the next 14 calendar days.)

6. Remember that you need a no in order to know. (If no one ever corrects you or tells you "This doesn't work," you can bet there's a problem with your information-gathering skills.)

7. Always get the prospect to do something. (People who are not committed to some form of action on your behalf are unlikely to deliver revenue. When in doubt, ask the person to meet with you, join a conference call, visit your office—anything!)

8. Never make a presentation you don't think will close. (If you have doubts about whether your proposal makes sense, get more information.)

9. Always have a fallback position. (Never stop asking yourself, "What do I do if . . . .?")

10. Do it in person. (Show up. Look the person in the eye. Don't get distracted by faxes, e-mail, and the latest software. Use it—but use it to support face-to-face human relationships.)

I believe that a book like this should be a beginning, not an ending. It should make you start asking yourself questions about what you're truly capable of achieving. I like to think that, over the years, we've helped more than our share of salespeople demand—and receive—the very best from themselves. We're not done yet, and I hope you aren't done either.

If you're interested in learning more about software based on the Prospect Management System, about how D.E.I. Management Group can help you improve your own sales performance or that of your team, or about our face-to-face training, contact us. Call 800-224-2140, visit us online at <www.dei-sales.com>, or drop me a line via e-mail at contactus@dei-sales.com.

Good luck!

ANSWERS TO CHAPTER QUIZZES

QUICK QUIZ: CHAPTER 1

1 (a)   2 (d)   3 (b)

QUICK QUIZ: CHAPTER 2

1 (b)   2 (a)

QUICK QUIZ: CHAPTER 3

1 (c)   2 (a)   3(c)

QUICK QUIZ: CHAPTER 4

1 (a)   2 (b)   3 (e)

QUICK QUIZ: CHAPTER 5

1 (a)

QUICK QUIZ: CHAPTER 6

1 (b)   2 (b)   3 (a)

QUICK QUIZ: CHAPTER 7

1 (b)   2 (a)   3 (b)

QUICK QUIZ: CHAPTER 8

1 (b)

QUICK QUIZ: CHAPTER 9

1 (a)   2 (b)   3 (c)

QUICK QUIZ: CHAPTER 10

1 (b) (e) (g) (h) (j)   2 (b) [Remember that people who sell over the phone can have 50 percent prospects, too!]   3 (d)

QUICK QUIZ: CHAPTER 11

1 (b) [They must meet all of the requirements for 50 percent prospect *and* give you a verbal commitment to do business.]   2 (c)   3 (c)

QUICK QUIZ: CHAPTER 12

1 (a)   2 (b)   3 (c)

QUICK QUIZ: CHAPTER 13

1 (e)   2 (d)   3 (a)   4 (b)   5 (c)   6 (a)

QUICK QUIZ: CHAPTER 14

1 (d)   2 (b)   3 (b)

QUICK QUIZ: CHAPTER 16

1 (b)   2 (d)   3 (c)

QUICK QUIZ: CHAPTER 17

1 (b)   2 (b)   3 (b)

QUICK QUIZ: CHAPTER 18

1 (a)   2 (d)

A

Your Monday Morning Sales Meeting

A Guide for Sales Managers

WHAT KINDS OF QUESTIONS ARE YOU ASKING REPS?

What kinds of questions are you asking your people during sales meetings? Do the questions you ask concern *when people are meeting next* with prospects? Do the questions you ask focus on *what the next step is and how to get it?*

We have a saying: Salespeople will do what you review. This means that salespeople have a way of preparing for what they know you're going to ask them about every week. If you make a habit of asking, "When are you going back?" people will make a habit of asking their prospects when they can come back!

It's important to put your questions during sales meetings in context. If you don't suggest ways to help to interpret the results of their activity, offer to help move the process forward yourself (see Chapter 17), and ask focused questions that clearly connect with both short-term and long-term success, your interactions won't be perceived as helpful.

We strongly suggest that you make a habit of gathering your team at least weekly to brainstorm and ask critical questions about each rep's activity and current prospects. For us, the meeting takes place *every Monday* without fail. We think you should consider scheduling your team's meeting in the same time slot. It's a great way to start the week.

REMEMBER. . . .

To get the most out of your weekly sales meetings, you and your team must implement D.E.I.'s definition of the word *prospect*.

A prospect is someone who is willing to give you a next step—with a specific time and date—to discuss the possibility of working with you. It's also important to remember that *prospects take action within our average selling cycle. So if your average selling cycle is four weeks, and you've got a next step with someone for eight weeks from now, don't put that person in the active prospect section of the system!*

Make a habit of asking your team the most important questions—so they can learn to ask the questions themselves instinctively.

KEY POINT: Habits are built up—and reinforced—through repetition. That means you and your team will get the most value from the ideas in *Getting to "Closed"* if you ask the same kinds of questions on a regular basis during weekly meetings.

ASK ABOUT PROSPECTS

As we have just reviewed, a sales rep who has no next step with a scheduled date and time *has no prospect.*

As you learned in Chapter 5, *salespeople must set a target for the number of appointments they set and active prospects they carry.*

In order for your sales team to perform at the highest level, you must ask questions that root out people who aren't really prospects, and then hold salespeople accountable for the number of prospects they actually maintain. Note again, with benefit to your career and your organization's competitive position, that we are urging you to monitor the person's total active prospects, not just the total closes.

How many real prospects are there on the person's board? Does the total number of real prospects on the board support the person's income goals, or not?

> **KEY POINT:** Most sales managers hold reps accountable for the *end result*—the total number of closed sales. Effective sales managers hold reps accountable for the *activity that delivers those results* by rooting out dead leads and emphasizing strict quotas for dials and active prospects.

Use questions to make a clear distinction between people who are interested in talking with your salespeople about working with your company and people who aren't. For every "new lead" a salesperson claims to have, ask:

- When did you first meet with this person about this sale?
- When are you meeting this person next?
- What does the company do? Who are its customers?
- When was the last time you met with this person?
- Is the time between meetings longer than normal for a sale this size?

After reviewing all prospects:

- How many total prospects do you really have?
- How close is that to your target?

> **KEY POINT:** Make sure your reps set and maintain a target number of new active prospects at all times. The number should support their weekly, monthly, and quarterly income goals. (At our company, reps are expected to set at least one new FA every day.)

ASK ABOUT KEY DEFINITIONS

In the best of all possible worlds, get your salespeople to attend Prospect Management training or read this book.

Failing that, share the following definitions with your team members. Set up a handout and demand that people memorize the terms. *Drill your team on the definitions until they're second nature.*

A *prospect* is someone who is willing to give you a next step with a specific time and date to discuss the possibility of working with you.

An *opportunity* is someone with whom you want to work, but who has not given you a next step with a specific date and time.

A *fallback* is someone who used to be an active prospect but now isn't.

Most salespeople believe they have many prospects. In fact, they have many opportunities. Opportunities are great, but your people shouldn't count on them for income within the current sales cycle.

REVIEW 50 PERCENT PROSPECTS CLOSELY

As you've learned, not all prospects are alike. The key prospects are the ones we call 50 percent prospects. These are prospects we have learned a good deal about; prospects who are considering us seriously. If the prospect reaches this point, we have a 50-50 chance to close the sale.

If your reps know nothing else about the categories of the Getting to Closed System, they should know that to get to 50 percent, they must be talking to the *real* decision maker about *real* dollars and a *real* timeline.

This is the yes-or-no point.

As a practical matter, sales meetings tend to follow this pattern: Quick review of 90 percent (verbal commitment) prospects, in-depth review and discussion of 50 percent prospects, group strategy blitz for appropriate 25 percent prospects. The moral: *Review 50 percent prospects closely.*

Among other things, ask these questions about leads your salespeople categorize as 50 percent prospects.

- Is this the decision maker? (How do you know? How did this person make the decision last time? Who else is likely to be involved?)
- Does what you are proposing fit into what this person/ organization is already doing? (How do you know? Was your proposal/recommendation/plan based on verbatim feedback from the prospect? Why did you recommend what you did?)
- How much is this deal worth? (If you don't know, then the prospect won't know how much to pay! *Only* prospects with whom you have discussed pricing are considered 50 percent prospects.)
- What's the timetable? (When will a decision be made? When will delivery/implementation take place? A decision one way or the other should be at hand! Usually, that means

we know we're going to get a yes or a no within a couple of weeks at the most.)

- When are you meeting with this person next? (What's the next step?)
- What does this person think will happen next? (How do you know? At the end of the meeting, did you say something like, "Listen, just between you and me, do you think I have a shot here?" If not, why not?)

You should know how many 50 percent prospects your team has at any given time. Set a target total for the team. *Root out contacts that aren't really 50 percent prospects.*

Point to ponder. Many a sale has closed quickly in our organization because a rep set out to prove to a manager that a given prospect *really* belonged at 50 percent, rather than 25 percent. We pass this information along to you for whatever it's worth, which may actually be quite a bit of money. Do whatever it takes to motivate your reps!

ASK ABOUT PROSPECTS IN MOTION

Your team's prospect base is dynamic. That means it is constantly in motion.

People are either moving toward a commitment to do business with you or away from that kind of commitment.

Constantly ask yourself and your team, "Are we moving toward a verbal commitment to do business with this person or are we falling off the person's radar screen?"

This question applies to any FA, 25 percent, or 50 percent prospect. Ask it!

If the salesperson tells you he or she is moving toward verbal commitment with the contact, ask how, specifically, he or she knows!

CHALLENGE THE REPS

Someone who was once an active prospect but has stopped playing ball with us, must be recategorized as an opportunity.

During the weekly team meeting, be ruthless in distinguishing (and omitting from consideration) any former prospect with whom your sales rep has not established a next step. If the contact will not set a time to meet or talk with your rep, he or she must be removed from the group of active prospects.

Discussions about whether or not a formerly "hot" lead really is an active prospect are good opportunities to strategize with the salesperson. How can the team work together to move the relationship with the contact forward?

Reps may resist you on this point. Stand your ground. By insisting that a given contact without a next step is an opportunity, you may inspire the salesperson to prove you wrong by setting up a next step before the next Monday meeting! Again: Do whatever it takes to motivate people!

ASK ABOUT NEW REVENUE SOURCES

Ask questions about the specific activities that will help your team develop brand new prospects and customers. For instance:

- How many dials did you make last week? How many of those dials turned into discussions with decision makers? How many of those discussions turned into appointments?
- How many appointments do you typically need to generate one sale? How does your current level of activity translate into income for this month/quarter/year? How does that compare to your goal?
- What are you going to do differently this week in your prospecting routine? What specific numerical targets are

you going to track, hit, and be ready to discuss at the next meeting?

- What leads or opportunities exist near appointments you have scheduled for this week? (Be alert for ways to use travel commitments to generate new prospects.) Which nearby opportunities or fallbacks can you talk to before or after your next scheduled meeting? If you leave a first appointment without a next step, can you at least bring back contact information on three more opportunities to contact by phone?

Your sales reps may be tempted to waste time and effort on leads that are in "permanent pending" mode. They are much better off finding someone new to talk to.

If your team has not been tracking these numbers, make sure they start doing so now!

MANAGE TIME EFFECTIVELY: IDENTIFY YOUR TEAM'S SELLING CYCLE

Each of your reps must learn to prioritize time—that is, devote more energy toward prospects who are progressively moving *toward* a decision to work with your company. As they do, they must become aware of their own sales cycle—the amount of time it typically takes them to close a sale. In our industry, the sales training industry, the cycle is about eight weeks. That's how long it takes us, on average, to move from a first appointment to a closed deal.

Why is it important to know what *your* company's selling cycle is? Because knowing the average selling cycle is one of the most important factors to an individual rep's sales success. This is because the *longer* any given set of discussions goes beyond your selling cycle, the *less* likely you are to close that sale.

Most reps don't realize this. They assume that the longer a set of discussions goes on, the *more* likely a deal is to come through. If only it were so! Once we reach the ninth week, we know the odds of our closing that sale have begun to drop, and we prioritize our efforts accordingly. Your team should do the same. Identify your team's average cycle, record the dates of first appointments, and then watch those numbers like a hawk!

Remember: There is an average amount of time it takes your sales rep to close a sale. There is also an average number of visits it takes your rep to close a sale. You must constantly monitor these time spans, and remind your reps to prioritize their day effectively. Tell your people, "Focus on people who are moving *toward* you, not away from you!"

ASK ABOUT KEY INFORMATION

Keep a record system that requires the reps to record the following information about each and every active prospect. Make sure they're ready to discuss all the elements at *any* time.

- Company name
- Date of first appointment (very important for comparing this lead to the average sales cycle)
- Dollar value (estimated value is fine in the early stages)
- Next step

Note: For more information about the Prospect Management System, visit <www.dei-sales.com> or call 800-224-2140.

ASK HOW LONG THE PROSPECT HAS BEEN PENDING

The date of your rep's first appointment, meeting, or in-depth discussion with the prospect is vitally important. That's when the sales cycle "clock" starts running!

Before we computerized our system, we transferred relevant information about all active leads onto small cards. These cards were fitted onto magnetic casings and placed on a big Prospect Board that served as the focus of the Monday morning meeting.

At each Monday morning meeting, the person running the meeting placed a small dot on each card affixed to the board. Why did we do this? Well, our sales cycle is roughly eight weeks. If we saw a card that had eight or more dots, we knew that it had been on the board for eight or more weeks. That meant it exceeded our average selling cycle, and more often than not, that's enough of a reason for us to take it out of active consideration and alter our forecasts. The rep must now develop a new prospect to meet his or her personal target.

This process has a way of getting a sales rep's attention. That's good! The rep is now inspired to take action, figure out what's really going on in an account, and strategize with the team on how to move the sale forward.

ASK TOUGH QUESTIONS AND "MAKE NOISE" IN THE RELATIONSHIP

During the Monday morning meeting, each sales rep should be quizzed about the number and status of all active prospects on the board. Five particularly important areas to ask about are:

1. Who are the organization's customers, competitors, and key suppliers?

2. What do you think is going to happen next?
3. What does the prospect think will happen next? Why?
4. When will the decision be made? What is your fallback plan if the decision is no (or is delayed)?
5. How can we work as a team to find out what's really happening and/or move the sale forward?

KEY POINT: If the rep plans to close the sale at the next meeting, this fact should not come as a surprise to the prospect!

As the manager, you have a great opportunity to "make noise" in the relationship and find out where prospects really stand. Call up people who are on the fence and say, "I understand we're going to be doing business together!" You'll immediately find out where the prospect stands.

MORE IMPORTANT QUESTIONS TO CONSIDER

More questions you should be ready to ask during the Monday meeting include:

- Did they ever buy a product or service like ours before? If so, how did they make the decision?
- Do you think this will close? If yes, when? (Be sure to get a definite date and record it!)
- When did you first meet with/speak with this person?
- How many times have you been there/spoken with this person?
- What is the next step? (Get a date!)
- Why has so much time gone by? (If appropriate.)
- How are you going to move this forward?
- Why don't I call this person?
- Why don't I go on your next meeting with this person?

- What else can we do to get the person to play ball with us? (Consider: invitations to company events, meetings with technical experts or other key team members, tour of your company's facilities, meeting/discussion with a happy customer of yours, conference call, etc.)
- Who is the true decision maker? How did he or she get the job? What was he or she doing beforehand? How old is he or she? How long has he or she been with the company?
- Who is the president/owner? How long has the company been in business?
- Finally, look at the salesperson's opportunities. (These are leads that have fallen out of the active prospect grouping.) Ask, "What here is worth strategizing? How can we move that opportunity into the active prospect category?"

Board Ranking/
Questions Tool

Appendix B:
Board Ranking/Questions Tool

GETTING TO CLOSED™ SYSTEM RANKING AND QUESTIONS OVERVIEW

CRITERIA	0	FA	1/25%	2/50%	3/90%	C/100%
	No next step No decision expected soon	Scheduled first meeting (date and time).	Had FA—now have scheduled next step to gain information.	Presenting to right person with right presentation, right price, right timetable.	Verbal Contract on desk	Sold, closed
Ranking Questions	Why is there is no next step? What is happening within the next two weeks?	Is this the first meeting about this sale? Is the meeting set?	When was the first meeting? When was the last meeting? When is the next appointment?	What is the deal worth? Need specific dollar amount. When will they decide?	When will this plan close? Need definite date.	Sold, closed
Strategy Questions	What other companies that are most like our existing customers can we call on? Who do our customers buy from and sell to that we can call on? What percentage of our next opportunities are new customers, former customers and existing customers?	Are each day's appointments close together? Are there any leads right near any of these appointments which would make sense to meet on this trip? What next step (and fallback) strategy will you use at the end of these meetings?	What are other examples of similar success stories we've had? What will it take to move this prospect to 50 percent? How long will that take? What would the sale be worth? What/how/why/when does this company/organization do what it does? Why that company? How did they choose them? Is this company looking at any competitor? Why that company? Why should they change? What are the individual decision makers trying to accomplish? How can we help them do it better?	Why are you presenting this proposal? How do you know this person (or people) will be able to make this decision? When will they decide? What is their timetable for implementation? Who else are we competing against? Has the specific dollar amount been discussed? Has the specific plan been discussed? Do we have a date to present this? Do they want this sale as much as you do?	Can you schedule any FAs near these closing appointments? Does the prospect know they're closing? Is this meeting merely to close or to advance the sale by beginning implementation? What specific plan(s) has been selected? Do we have a verbal commitment to do business?	Sold, closed
Overall Board Management Questions	What are the next 11 opportunities to pursue and why? Are there other contacts within our existing prospects and customers worth pursuing?	What is the right number of FAs to maintain at all times?	What does this column tell us about our recent prospecting activity? A low number would indicate: 1. Not enough FAs in last two weeks. 2. Inability to create a next step with qualified prospects 3. Small size prospects which skipped the first stage. 4. Recent FAs were predominantly unqualified (either contact or organization). Is any prospect in this column too old? Do we have a one-in-four chance of closing these sales?	What resources/strategies can be utilized to drive these decisions? If we're waiting for a decision, can we also prospect for new business? Is the value of these prospects multiplied by 50 percent sufficient to hit short-term sales goals? What should the average prospect value be? If too high, the sales cycle lengthens; if too low, prospecting activity must increase. Is any prospect in this column too old? Is there a one-in-two chance of closing these sales?	Compared to the 50 percent column, does this column indicate closing skills, presentation or ranking problems? Is any prospect in this column too old? Do we have a 90 percent chance of closing these sales?	What are the next opportunities within these accounts for more sales? When should these opportunities be pursued?

Note:
Shading indicates ideal board configuration.

Contact Categorization Exercise

The scenarios you're about to read are an integral part of D.E.I.'s in-person training program.

Assume your average selling cycle is eight weeks. In which category of the Getting to Closed™ system does each contact belong?

(Answers appear at the end of this appendix.)

1. WALSH & CO.

PROSPECT MANAGEMENT SYSTEM™

Date	Appts.
	I called Mike Waters, office manager at this local publishing firm; set meeting for next week.
1 wk. later	I met with Mike and learned that Walsh & Co. is using ABC Company for service now.
	Mike is looking for better pricing as well as easier access when service issues come up.
	He is "sick of being put on hold and leaving messages that don't get returned," Mike said
	Walsh's CFO had selected ABC three years ago. He did not know what had gone into
	that decision. I asked more questions, took notes, and asked if I could meet with Mike again
	next Tuesday at 2:00. He agreed.
2 wks. later	I presented my proposal to Mike. He said it "looked good" and that he wanted to discuss it with
	the CFO. He said he would call me within two weeks.
3 wks. later	Called Mike. He said the CFO had not made a decision. Promised to call when he had more info.

This contact should be categorized as _____.

2. YEE UNLIMITED

PROSPECT MANAGEMENT SYSTEM™

Date	Appts.
	Called Bob Yee, owner of this promotional item manufacturer; set meeting for 2 days from now.
2 days later	Met with Bob and asked how he planned to expand his business. Learned he is hoping to improve service and delivery time to his customers. He said he was "looking for help."
	I asked questions, took notes, and set an appointment to meet with Bob 3 days from now.
3 days later	I delivered a proposal that outlined cost savings and projected service and delivery improvements. Bob was very impressed, especially with my assurance that he could call me personally at any time—at home or at work—to discuss the plan's implementation and give feedback. Four days later, I received his signed contract.

This contact should be categorized as _____.

3. FLYNN RESEARCH

PROSPECT MANAGEMENT SYSTEM™

Date	Appts.
	I stopped in at this legal research firm and asked to speak to the president, Mike Flynn. His
	assistant said Mike was busy, but arranged an appointment for next week.
1 wk. later	I met with Mike, found out how the firm conducted its business, and learned that Flynn
	Research was using Acme, our competitor. Mike said he was unhappy with Acme's performance;
	he asked me to prepare a proposal. We discussed timelines and the kind of plan he wanted
	to see, but when I asked what kind of budget he was working with, Mike asked that we
	discuss that later. I gathered more information about how Flynn had chosen Acme in the first
	place and what had gone wrong since. I set an appointment for the following week.
1 wk. later	I delivered my proposal; stayed away from any pricing until I could get more info from Mike,
	who was in a rush. I could not get another meeting, as it was the company's busy season. But,
	Mike said he "loved" our recommendation and would make a point of calling me next week.

This contact should be categorized as _____.

4. MILLER COMMUNICATIONS

PROSPECT MANAGEMENT SYSTEM™

Date	Appts.
	I called Becky Miller, the owner of this P.R. firm, from a client referral and set an appointment for two days from now.
Two days later	I met with Becky and found out how she founded the business ten years ago. We discussed her goals: she wants to expand her staff and attract significantly more *Fortune* 500 companies as clients. We discussed Becky's budget and plans: She aims to open another office next year. I learned that Becky was using Acme Corporation, a competitor of ours. I asked how she decided to work with Acme. She said she had received the recommendation from her brother-in-law, who once worked at Acme. I set a meeting with Becky to return in two days to "get her reaction to my preliminary outline for a formal proposal.

This contact should be categorized as: _____ .

5. SMITH & CO.

PROSPECT MANAGEMENT SYSTEM™

Date	Appts.
	I called Jack Harvey, the owner of this small chain of retail stores, from a newspaper
	lead. I set a meeting for two days from now.
2 days later	I met with Jack and learned that Smith currently uses Acme, our competitor, but is looking
	for a more sophisticated package. I learned why Jack chose Acme in the first place and how
	he has evaluated its performance over the last three years. I learned that his marketing
	goals over the next three months will require considerably quicker turnaround than Acme has
	been able to provide. I suggested I return in three days with a proposal based on our discussion;
	Jack agreed.
3 days later	I made the presentation; Jack was impressed. He asked me to come back next Monday at 2:00.
1 wk. later	Jack said he would go with us; he is reviewing contract. Tentative start date has been set.

This contact should be categorized as _____.

6. CRUZ & ASSOCIATES

PROSPECT MANAGEMENT SYSTEM™

Date	Appts.
	I called the president of this local accounting firm and set a meeting for three weeks from now.
3 wks. later	I met with Heloise Cruz, the president. I learned her firm was losing market share to a large competitor and was eager to find ways to reverse that trend. I found out all I could about what Heloise is trying to accomplish in this market and what her history of working with companies like ours is. I asked to meet again with Heloise to gather more information. It turns out that Heloise is busy for the next 90–120 days with internal matters, so I set an appointment with her for a little over four months from today, on a Monday at 10:00 AM

This contact should be categorized as _____.

7. BERNINI CASUALS

PROSPECT MANAGEMENT SYSTEM™

Date	Appts.
	I called Mia Bernini, owner of this chain of fashion outlets; set an appointment for tomorrow. I met
1 day later	with Mia and learned that she was struggling with a downturn in her market. I set the next meeting.
1 wk. later	Mia is considering a campaign to reach an entirely new group of customers. She has never worked
	with a company like ours before. We discussed pricing, timelines, and implementation. We had an
	excellent meeting that lasted for nearly an hour. I filled most of a yellow legal pad with
	Mia's answers to my questions. "If I were going to look at a proposal," she told me,
	"I'd want it to address specific timelines, past histories of similar campaigns, and a budget under
	$15,000 over the first 60 days." I told Mia I felt confident I could assemble such
	a proposal. She agreed to meet with me next Tuesday at 1:00 to see what I'd come up with.

This contact should be categorized as _____.

8. MCQUICKLEY SYSTEMS

PROSPECT MANAGEMENT SYSTEM™

Date	Appts.
	I left a message for Dirk McQuickley, the owner and founder of the company, who was in a meeting.
1 wk. later	I called Dirk again and set an appointment for next Tuesday at 2:00 pm to learn about McQuickley Systems' operations, and about possible applications for our products and services.

This contact should be categorized as _____.

9. VOMOV.COM

PROSPECT MANAGEMENT SYSTEM™

Date	Appts.
	I left a message for Ryan Vomov, the owner and founder of this online retailer,
	who was in a meeting. I got no response.
1 wk. later	I called Ryan again and suggested a meeting next Tuesday at 2:00 pm to learn about
	Vomov.com's operations, and about possible applications for our products and
	services. Ryan was extremely enthusiastic, and said he "was hoping to get a call like this."
	Ryan was preparing for a trade show and, thus, could not agree to meet next Tuesday. He did,
	however, say that meeting with me after the show would be his "top priority," and
	promised to have his assistant phone soon with the date and time of our meeting.

This contact should be categorized as _____ .

10. ROUGHHOUSE CLOTHING

PROSPECT MANAGEMENT SYSTEM™

Date	Appts.
	I cold called and set a meeting with Max Day, office manager of this local clothing firm.
1 wk. later	I met with Max and learned that he and the president of the company had selected the current vendor, our competitor Acme Corporation. Max has been with Roughhouse for ten years.
	After a few minutes of small talk, I immediately explained in depth why we were superior to Acme. Max said very little during the meeting. I asked whether I could meet again with Max and the president of the organization. Max said the president was on vacation and no one was sure when he would be back, but that he would be sure to call me when the next slot opened up. He thought that might be sometime next month.

This contact should be categorized as _____.

ANSWERS FOR APPENDIX C

1. Fallback/opportunity
2. Closed
3. Fallback/opportunity
4. 25 percent
5. 90 percent
6. Fallback/opportunity (the next step is in place, but it is set for a point well beyond your average selling cycle)
7. 50 percent
8. FA
9. Fallback/opportunity
10. Fallback/opportunity

If you misidentified even one of these ten scenarios, you have not yet mastered the Getting to Closed system!

Sales Scenarios

Assume that you're a sales rep for a major telecommunications provider. Rank the following four contacts from 1 to 4, with the most promising scenario ranked first. (Answer appears at the end of this appendix.)

SCENARIO A: FORRESTER AND TWOMBLY

HIGH EFFICIENCY SELLING SKILLS™

Assume your average selling cycle is *eight weeks* after the first meeting or in-depth conversation.

About the company: Forrester and Twombly is one of the top law firms in the area. It has five offices in three states and over 100 employees.

Chronology

- During a brief phone call, I set an appointment for three days from now with the office manager at Forrester and Twombly's main office, Roberto Gonzales.
- I met for approximately 15 minutes with Roberto and asked him what, if anything, he would change about his firm's current phone and Internet arrangements. Roberto said he couldn't think of anything that was a problem. He had no questions for me, so I reviewed TeleConnect's entire range of products. Then Roberto told me he had to prepare for a meeting and asked that I give him a call "sometime next week."
- *Two weeks after first appointment:* I tried and failed to reach Roberto. I meant to call the previous week, but things had been hectic. I received no return call.
- *Four weeks after first appointment:* I reached Roberto by phone and learned that he was planning a companywide review of the company's communications program, and would be meeting with key personnel at each of the company's five offices next month to discuss the selection of a new provider. I asked for the chance to make a 15-minute presentation at that meeting. Roberto agreed to let me attend, but asked that I keep it to five minutes. He mentioned that he and Daniel

Lewis, the new assistant to the firm's senior partner, would be making the final selection of a new vendor.

- *Eight weeks after first appointment:* I sat in on Roberto's meeting to discuss Forrester's future phone, data, and Internet service. At the beginning of the meeting, I learned that Daniel Lewis was out sick that day, and that quick, reliable videoconferencing was a priority for all the firm's attorneys. At the beginning of the discussion, I made a five-minute "pitch" that emphasized TeleConnect's high-speed Internet access, which I knew had been important to another law firm in the area that eventually bought from us. At the conclusion of my "floor time," Roberto asked that I give the team time to meet privately. I asked if we could connect next week, and he agreed.
- *Nine weeks after first appointment:* I followed up with Roberto via phone; he told me the group had enjoyed my presentation, but that Daniel Lewis was now taking the lead in evaluating vendors. I told Roberto that I would follow up with Daniel, whom I had not yet met.
- *Ten weeks after first appointment:* I left a message for Daniel and told him that Roberto had suggested I call.

Instructions: Fill in the blank below.

This sequence ranks ___ out of four, with one being the most promising. Then:

Circle the high point of this sequence (if you find one).
Place an **X** by the low point of this sequence (if you find one).

SCENARIO B: BIG CITY TOURS

HIGH EFFICIENCY SELLING SKILLS™

Assume your average selling cycle is *eight weeks* after the first meeting or in-depth conversation.

About the company: Big City Tours provides visitors and locals with historic tours of the city. They have two offices and 100 employees.

Chronology

- I cold called Karen Hansen, the office manager of Big City Tours, and made an appointment for the following week.
- I met with Karen and learned about Big City's phone and data services; I learned that there was a number of different providers. I asked how these vendors had been chosen. Karen said she wasn't sure because she had only recently become office manager of the company. When I asked about what she had done prior to joining Big City Tours, Karen said she had worked as the office manager of a competing tourist company. Big City's owner had personally recruited her to join the company. Karen was intrigued by the possibility of streamlining service, reducing downtime, and cutting costs. She agreed to meet with me next Tuesday at 2:00, and promised to fax sample bills to me tomorrow. (She wasn't sure where the files for past bills were located.)
- *Three days after first meeting:* I called Karen back and asked if she'd had the chance to locate the bills we'd discussed. She apologized for the delay and promised to fax them to me that afternoon. She did so. I analyzed the bills.
- *One week after first meeting:* I met with Karen again and learned that service was a major concern of hers. Past service and connection problems related to her company's voice and data services had already made her relationship

with her new boss difficult—and Karen had only been on the job for four weeks. I briefly described TeleConnect's support philosophy. Our discussion was interrupted when the president of Big City Tours asked Karen if she could meet with him immediately to discuss an urgent issue. Karen said she would call me back tomorrow; I suggested 2:00 PM, and she agreed.

- *One week and one day after first meeting:* Karen called back as promised. Over the phone, she told me that one of her company's most important goals was to improve relations with out-of-state organizations planning tours. I talked about TeleConnect's prepaid calling cards and explained how other organizations had used these effectively as promotional items. I also pointed out that TeleConnect could help Big City Tours become more accessible to out-of-state customers by establishing a toll-free business number, as we had done for Beacon Gifts. I set a meeting for next week.

- *Two weeks after first meeting:* I met with Karen and reviewed an outline of the customized solution I was considering for her company. We discussed pricing and timetables for implementation. I asked Karen if there was anyone else who would need to part of the decision-making process. She said that Ike Rossi, the president, would evaluate whether to switch their vendors. I set an appointment with Karen and Ike for ten days from now to continue the process.

Instructions: Fill in the blank below.

This sequence ranks ___ out of four, with one being the most promising. Then:

(Circle) the high point of this sequence (if you find one).

Place an **X** by the low point of this sequence (if you find one).

SCENARIO C: NEW IMAGE

HIGH EFFICIENCY SELLING SKILLS™

Assume your average selling cycle is *eight weeks* after the first meeting or in-depth conversation.

About the company: New Image is an advertising agency that specializes in edgy, high-energy print and broadcast campaigns targeting people 20 years old and younger. They have four offices on the West Coast and employ 250 people.

Chronology

- I made three unsuccessful attempts to reach the president, Nigel Hammond, on the phone. Finally, I spoke with his secretary and scheduled a meeting for one week later.
- I met with Nigel. I asked him if he was satisfied with his current phone and Internet service. He said he was pleased most of the time, but that there had been a period recently when he had had problems connecting to the Internet. We discussed what TeleConnect Business Communications had to offer. Nigel said I would have to speak to Suzanne Martin, the VP of Operations, who was on vacation that week. He gave me a stack of recent bills to review. That afternoon, I called Suzanne and set a meeting for three days later.
- *Three days after first appointment:* I met briefly with Suzanne. She said she was working with Nigel on streamlining the company's communications program and improving ease of connectivity between the various offices. She mentioned that it was "lucky" that I called when I did because the company was currently in "search mode" for a new provider. I asked if she had anything in particular that she wanted to know about TeleConnect; she said that I should simply "take it from the top." I went through a brief demonstration of how TeleConnect's services could improve connection

speed, increase efficiency, and lower costs compared to what she had in place now. Suzanne seemed interested, but said I would have to meet with her and Nigel again to go over the details. I made an appointment for two weeks later to present a proposal.

- *A week and a half after first appointment:* I received a phone call from Suzanne explaining that she and Nigel would need to reschedule their appointment because she was tied up with business trips for the next month. She suggested that she call next month when her schedule cleared up; I agreed.
- *Five and a half weeks after first appointment:* I called and set a new appointment. When I met with Suzanne and Nigel, I presented a comprehensive proposal and explained how we could streamline New Image's communications program and save them money. Suzanne and Nigel said they needed time to discuss the proposal and would get back to me within two weeks.
- *Seven and a half weeks after first appointment:* I called Nigel, who said another organization had just presented another plan to him. He suggested that he compare both proposals and get back to me "in a few weeks." I said I thought that would be fine.

Instructions: Fill in the blank below.

This sequence ranks ___ out of four, with one being the most promising.
Then:

    Circle the high point of this sequence (if you find one).
Place an **X** by the low point of this sequence (if you find one).

SCENARIO D: BRIGHT MEDICAL

HIGH EFFICIENCY SELLING SKILLS™

Assume your average selling cycle is *eight weeks* after the first meeting or in-depth conversation.

About the company: Bright Medical is a supplier of surgical and rehabilitation equipment suppliers. Their customers are locally based hospitals.

Chronology

- I left a message for Arthur Krug, the office manager. He returned my call a day later and we set up a meeting for next week.
- I met with Arthur. After some preliminary talk about his career and his role at Bright, I asked him to describe the projects that were of top priority to him. Arthur said that Bright Medical was looking to expand sales into surrounding regions and to enlarge its sales force. Of greater immediate importance, were several urgent problems related to complaints about some of his new products. As a result, Arthur's goal of selecting a new voice and data service provider was no longer the highest priority. Arthur briefly introduced me to the president of the company, Mike Bright. Mike mentioned that the selection of voice and data service providers was exclusively "Arthur's call." Later, Arthur informed me that there were contractual restrictions related to the current provider, but that he wasn't sure what they were and had no time to look the contracts up now. Before leaving, I made an appointment in ten days to talk with Arthur again.
- *Ten days after first appointment:* I met with Arthur again and learned that there were many networking and Internet opportunities where I felt TeleConnect could add value and

improve service. Before excusing himself to attend a companywide meeting, Arthur gave me the company's telecom bills for the past 90 days. Arthur told me to set up an appointment with his assistant, Cheryl; the first available slot was next week.

- *Two and a half weeks after first appointment:* I reviewed my preliminary proposal with Arthur, who said it "looked very good," but asked me to try to develop a better pricing approach. Arthur also informed me that, due to contractual obligations, he would not be able to switch over to a new company for at least 60 days. Arthur again referred me to Cheryl to set up another appointment. Due to a trade show that is taking place next week and Arthur's impending vacation, the soonest I could schedule a meeting was for one month from today.

Instructions: Fill in the blank below.

This sequence ranks ___ out of four, with one being the most promising. Then:

    Circle the high point of this sequence (if you find one).

    Place an **X** by the low point of this sequence (if you find one).

REASONS FOR THE RANKINGS

Scenario A: Forrester and Twombly

This should be ranked *4 out of 4.*

At the first meeting, the representative asked what, if anything, Roberto would change about his firm's current phone and Internet arrangements. *Poor initial questioning strategy.*

The representative reported that Roberto had no questions, so the rep reviewed TeleConnect's entire range of products. *Product dump.*

The representative meant to call the previous week, but things had been "hectic." *Poor follow-through.*

The representative reported that Roberto mentioned that he and Daniel Lewis, the new assistant to the firm's senior partner, would be making the final selection of a new vendor. *The representative makes no effort to meet with, talk to, or establish contact with new decision maker. Ideally, the meeting would involve rep, initial contact, and new player.*

The representative reports: "At the beginning of the meeting, I learned . . . that quick, reliable videoconferencing was a priority for all the firm's attorneys. At the beginning of the discussion, I made a five-minute 'pitch' that emphasized TeleConnect's high-speed Internet access, which I knew had been important to another law firm in the area that eventually bought from us." *Representative emphasizes element of service package that does not focus on prospect's key concern, namely videoconferencing.*

"I told Roberto that I would follow up with Daniel." *The representative fails again even to attempt to secure a face-to-face meeting involving himself, his contact, and Daniel Lewis.*

Finally, notice that the sales cycle, as the scenario closes, has extended to ten weeks past the first meeting. The average cycle for a prospect who decides to buy, we have assumed, is eight weeks past the first meeting.

Scenario B: Big City Tours

This should be ranked *1 out of 4.*

"When I asked about what she had done prior to joining Big City Tours, Karen said she had worked as the office manager of a competing tourist company. Big City's owner had personally recruited her to join the company." *Good questioning; important information results from queries about prospect's personal career history.*

"I called Karen back and asked if she'd had the chance to locate the bills we'd discussed." *Proactive follow-through; representative does not wait to hear from busy prospect, but makes a tactful call to obtain essential information.*

"Karen said she would call me back tomorrow; I suggested 2:00 PM, and she agreed." *The representative suggests specific time for next contact.*

"I also pointed out that TeleConnect could help Big City Tours become more accessible to out-of-state customers by establishing a toll-free business number, as we had done for Beacon Gifts." *Effective use of success story.*

"I met with Karen and reviewed an outline of the customized solution I was considering for her company." *Representative uses outline to verify information before making any formal recommendation.*

"I set an appointment with Karen and Ike for ten days from now to continue the process." *Representative sets next step involving both current contact and head of company.*

Finally, note that sale is unfolding within the average sales cycle.

Scenario C: New Image

This should be ranked *3 out of 4*. (This scenario ranks slightly higher than the Forrester and Twombly scenario, because here, at least, the representative is in fact talking to both of the key people in the company.)

"I met with Nigel. I asked him if he was satisfied with his current phone and Internet service." *Poor initial questioning strategy.*

"She mentioned that it was 'lucky' that I called when I did because the company was currently in 'search mode' for a new provider. I asked if she had anything in particular that she wanted to know about TeleConnect." *No attempt to find out what has recently changed in the prospect's world. Why has New Image decided to go into "search mode"?*

"I received a phone call from Suzanne explaining that she and Nigel would need to reschedule their appointment because she was tied up with business trips for the next month. She suggested that she call next month when her schedule cleared up; I agreed." *No attempt to set specific date and time for next meeting.*

"I presented a comprehensive proposal and explained how we could streamline New Image's communications program and save them money. *Because only a "brief demonstration" has preceded this meeting, and because questioning about what is actually going on at New Image has been superficial at best, a condensed outline would have been more appropriate than a "comprehensive proposal." Such an outline would have given Nigel and Suzanne the opportunity to correct and refine the sales rep's assumptions. This step should precede a formal recommendation.*

"He suggested that he compare both proposals and get back to me "in a few weeks." I said I thought that would be fine." *No attempt to determine whether a competitor contacted the prospect or vice versa; no attempt to set a next step.*

Scenario D: Bright Medical

This should be ranked *2 out of 4*. (This scenario ranks *lower* than the Big City Tours scenario because it is certain to exceed the average sales cycle. This lead ranks *higher* than Forrester and Twombly or New Image, however, because the representative has developed a plan that appears to make sense to the actual decision maker. Bright Medical could indeed be classified as inactive for the time being, given the contractual obstacles and the long timeline; a great deal could still go wrong. If this lead were to be regarded as inactive, however, it would still be an excellent fallback or opportunity. Forrester and Twombly and New Image, by contrast, look suspiciously like dead ends.)

"I met with Arthur. After some preliminary talk about his career and his role at Bright, I asked him to describe the projects that were of top priority to him." *Sound initial questioning strategy.*

"Arthur briefly introduced me to the president of the company, Mike Bright; Mike mentioned that the selection of voice and data service providers was exclusively 'Arthur's call.'" *Strong indication that representative is dealing with final decision maker.*

"Before leaving, I made an appointment in ten days to talk with Arthur again." *Establishment of next step.*

"Arthur gave me the company's telecom bills for the past 90 days. Arthur told me to set up an appointment with his assistant, Cheryl; the first available slot was next week." Clear signs of buy-in from prospect. The representative sets a next step before leaving the first face-to-face meeting.

"I reviewed my preliminary proposal with Arthur, who said it 'looked very good,' but asked me to try to develop a better pricing approach . . . . Due to a trade show that is taking place next week and Arthur's impending vacation, the soonest I could schedule a meeting was for one month from today. Contact is still "playing ball." Next step is in place, but this lead now exceeds the average selling cycle.

The Prospect Management Board and Time Management

By constantly monitoring all the current activity on your board, you will reinforce solid time management habits. Using it to view your prospecting, interviewing, presentation, and closing work *as part of the sales cycle,* rather than as isolated tasks to be entered onto your to-do list as time allows, means you can use the Prospect Board to get a snapshot of your activity. This snapshot will reveal how all your work is paying off.

Your best weekly schedule will arise in a natural way from the work you do on your Prospect Board. Each Friday afternoon, use your board to set your schedule for the following week. Start from the prospecting phase—remember, prospecting is the engine that drives the whole process—and move forward from there. Break all of your activities into one of the following eight categories, *in the following priority:*

1. Calls or e-mails to new contacts
2. First appointments with new contacts
3. Work that helps you move people from the 90 percent column into the closed column

4. Work that helps you move people in the 50 percent column into the 90 percent column

5. Work that helps you move people from the 25 percent column into the 50 percent column

6. Service calls and support work for recently closed sales and existing accounts

7. Special projects/administrative work (This includes sales reports, paperwork, or task force projects.)

8. Other/personal (This includes time off, medical appointments, and other commitments that will have an impact on your week.)

Everything you do on the job as a salesperson should be grouped into one of the above categories. Use the special Strategy and Action Planning Sheet like the one that follows to coordinate it all.

The Strategy and Action Planning Sheet combines your board and your personal calendar into a single tool that will help you plan your day for success. It shows you how your work has to be scheduled. Here's how to use it.

First, *fill in the top columns* with your prospect commitments, commitments to current customers, next steps, ongoing tasks, and new projects—all the things you want to work on over the next two weeks. Do not assign time slots; those go in the lower columns. Consult your Prospect Board first and your personal calendar second. Note: Because the evaluation process takes place on a weekly basis, but incorporates two weeks at a time, the week you're *about* to start will inevitably benefit from a second draft of your schedule. When you schedule the week that's still one week away, you're developing a preliminary outline of what you want to work on—an outline you'll adjust next week. Be sure to include personal errands and anything else that may take time from selling and servicing your prospects and clients.

Second, *write in your key objectives* in the lower columns on the left-hand side. Specify what you want to accomplish this week.

Finally, *go through each of the lower columns* and schedule the appropriate activity for each time slot, using the upper columns as your guide. In particular, be sure to identify your daily prospecting targets. Again: *Enter these as your first priority.* Block out time to call and set appointments first. Then schedule items in all the other categories

An updated-weekly, two-weeks-ahead look into the future might look like the sample Strategy and Action Planning Sheet that follows the blank one.

If you maintain your Prospect Board and use the Strategy and Action Planning Sheet regularly, you'll have taken the first, and probably the most important, step toward assuming control of your working schedule and your own sales process.

Prospect Management Sales Strategy and Activity Worksheet

NEXT STEPS/STRATEGY STEPS	✗ = Scheduled Step		✓ = Done
Fallbacks/ Opportunity	First Appointment	1	2
— 1 _____	— 1 _____	— 1 _____	— 1 _____
— 2 _____	— 2 _____	— 2 _____	— 2 _____
— 3 _____	— 3 _____	— 3 _____	— 3 _____
— 4 _____	— 4 _____	— 4 _____	— 4 _____
— 5 _____	— 5 _____	— 5 _____	— 5 _____
— 6 _____	— 6 _____	— 6 _____	— 6 _____
— 7 _____	— 7 _____	— 7 _____	— 7 _____
— 8 _____	— 8 _____	— 8 _____	— 8 _____
— 9 _____	— 9 _____	— 9 _____	— 9 _____
— 10 _____	— 10 _____	— 10 _____	— 10 _____
— 11 _____	— 11 _____	— 11 _____	— 11 _____
— 12 _____	— 12 _____	— 12 _____	— 12 _____

PLANNING CALENDAR Hint: Include Travel Time, Research, Proposals, etc.

Week of ___ ___ ___ Key Objectives:	Early A.M.	MON	TUE
	A.M.		
	P.M.		
	Late P.M.		

Week of ___ ___ ___ Key Objectives:	Early A.M.	MON	TUE
	A.M.		
	P.M.		
	Late P.M.		

Reminder-Strategy Steps for Next Week _____ _____

_____ _____

_____ _____

	3	Close/Service	Special Projects/ Tasks	Other/Personal
1		1	1	1
2		2	2	2
3		3	3	3
4		4	4	4
5		5	5	5
6		6	6	6
7		7	7	7
8		8	8	8
9		9	9	9
10		10	10	10
11		11	11	11
12		12	12	12

WED	THU	FRI	SAT/SUN
		Plan Next Week	

WED	THU	FRI	SAT/SUN
		Plan Next Week	

A Sample Prospect Management Sales Strategy and Activity Worksheet Filled In

NEXT STEPS/STRATEGY STEPS   **X** = Scheduled Step   **✓** = Done

Fallbacks/ Opportunity	First Appointment	1	2
1 Becker, Inc.	1 Michelin, Inc.	1 Borden List	1 Phillips Co.
2 Fuller, Inc.	2 Hachette	2 Best Co.	2 Trapou Editing
3 Transport Co.	3 Miller & Co.	3 Harbor Inc.	3 Kaplan Tests
4 Lincoln Savings	4 Trenton Leasing	4 Armor Metals	4 Simmons
5 Freshest	5	5 Quick Edit	5
6 Freshest	6	6 Fast Track	6
7 Lawn Care Co.	7	7	7
8 Prescott.	8	8	8
9	9	9	9
10	10	10	10
11	11	11	11
12	12	12	12

PLANNING CALENDAR   Hint: Include Travel Time, Research, Proposals, etc.

Week of 12 1 98 **Key Objectives:** Get more first appt.	Early A.M.	Write Proposal Simmons **MON**	Michelin **TUE**
	A.M.	Make 15 appt. calls	Hachette
	P.M.	Hachette appt.	Write proposal for Tarapou
	Late P.M.	Haircut	

Week of 12 8 98 **Key Objectives:**	Early A.M.	Grand Health Installation **MON**	Simmons **TUE** Philly Shipments Service
	A.M.		
	P.M.	Make 15 appt. calls	Quick Edit
	Late P.M.		

Reminder-Strategy Steps for Next Week   _____   _____

_____   _____

	3		Close/Service	Special Projects/ Tasks		Other/Personal
1	Parker Hospital	1	Grand Health	1	Task Force Mfg.	1 Get haircut
2	Electrical Lights	2	Medical Partners	2	Quality Control	2 Regist. training
3		3	Philly Shipments	3	Manager Mfg.	3 Buy calendar
4		4		4	Calls	4
5		5		5		5
6		6		6		6
7		7		7		7
8		8		8		8
9		9		9		9
10		10		10		10
11		11		11		11
12		12		12		12

WED	**THU**	**FRI**	**SAT/SUN**
Make 15 appt. calls Medical Partners Service set-up	Call Parker Hospital Make 15 appt. calls	Call Armor Metals Make 15 appt. calls	
Quality Meeting	Best Co.	Torapau Plan Next Week	

WED	**THU**	**FRI**	**SAT/SUN**
Call Electrical	Kaplan Tests Borden List	Phillips Co.	
Harbor Inc. Miller & Co.	Trenton Leasing	Managers Meeting Plan Next Week	

Index

Active prospect(s), 66, 82
    50 percent column, 69–76, 86
    90 percent column, 77–80, 86
    review of, 108–9
    25 percent column, 81–84, 86
Active Prospect Selling, 27
Activity questions, 111
Alliance questions, 110
Appointments, 27, 39–40, 125
    first appointment column,
       63–67, 86
AT&T, 3
Average selling cycle, 33–35, 73, 87,
    89, 94

Board review, 107–12
Budget, 71, 72–73

Candidates, 48
Clearnet Inc., 121–23
Close
    closing ratio, 9
    "makes sense to me," 16–17
Closed category, 59–60, 87

Cold calls (dials), 7–8, 25
Company (board review) questions,
    110
Contacts
    board review questions, 110
    categorizing, 37–49
    see also Prospects/prospecting
Contract on Desk (C.O.D.), 78, 86

D.E.I. Management Group, 122–23,
    126
Decision-makers, finding, 14
Dials. *See* Cold calls (dials)
Dollars to total sales ratio, 9

Effective selling, defined, 12
Executive Sales Briefing, The, 121
Exxon-Mobil, 3

Face to face sales, 34–35
Fallbacks, 55, 86, 126
Federal Express, 3

50 percent column, 69–76, 86
  criteria, 70–72, 74–75
  pricing, 71, 72–73
  sales cycle and, 73
  sales diagnostic strategy, 73–74
First appointments, 63–67, 86, 88, 89
Forecasting, 117–19, 122

Income, anticipating, 118
Information gathering
  (interviewing), 11–13, 16, 19–20, 37,
  125
Interviewing step. See Information
  gathering (interviewing)

Law of Replacement, 35
Leads, 48
Lexis-Nexis, 3

"Makes sense to me" close, 16–17
MCI/World Com, 3
Merrill Lynch, 3
Motorola, 3
90 percent column, 77–80, 86

O'Brien, Tim, 122
One-third rule, 24
Opening, 11, 20
  inefficient, 20–21
Opportunities, 47–49, 86, 102
  fallbacks, 55
  opportunity column, 53–56

Pending proposal formation, 97
Presentation, 11, 20, 22, 23, 126
Pricing, 71, 72–73
Product dump, 21
Product knowledge (product
  malleability), 22, 23
Professional development, 22, 23
Prospect Board, 36
  deviations of, 94–98
  dynamic nature of, 103

review sessions, 107–12, 113
  see also Prospect Management
    System
Prospects/prospecting, 22, 23, 54, 122
  active prospects, 66
  appointments and, 39–40
  managing base of prospects,
    27–30. See also Prospect
    Management System
  narrowing definition of
    prospects, 46
  prospect status questions, 109
  replenishing prospect base, 35
  team selling, 113–16
  see also Contacts, categorizing
Prospect Management System, 3–4,
  35–37, 126
  analyzing selling cycle with, 94
  applying to existing business,
    101
  board reviews, 107–12
  case studies, 121–23
  closed column, 59–60
  common questions, 101–3
  defined, 35–36
  50 percent column, 69–76
  first appointment column, 63–67
  forecasting, 117–19
  90 percent column, 77–80
  opportunity column, 53–56, 86,
    102
  reevaluating, 93–98
  25 percent column, 81–84, 86
  see also Prospect Board

Ratios
  monitoring and improving, 8–9
  "no" answers, counting, 25–26
  20:5:1, 25
Reclamation strategies, 113–15
Referrals, 48–49
Revenue, anticipating, 118

Sales diagnostic strategy, 73–74
Sales manager, 114

Sales process
  average selling cycle, estimating,
    33–35
  four P's, 22–23
  four steps of, 9–11, 15–17, 19–20
  inefficient model, 20–22
  information gathering, 11–13, 16,
    19–20, 125
  monitoring sales numbers,
    39–42
  one-third rule, 24
  presentation, 11, 20, 22, 23, 126
  prospecting. *See* Prospects/
    prospecting
  questions and forward
    movement of, 14
  ratios, monitoring and
    improving, 8–9
  rescuing "lost" sales, 113–16
  status quo, 13–14
  success principles, 125–26
  time and, 15, 87–89

Schiffman, Steve, 4, 64
Selling cycle, 33–35, 73, 87–89
  analyzing, 94
Slapshot responses, 21–22
Software, Prospect Management, 37
Sprint, 3
Status quo, 13–14
Stephan Schiffman's Telemarketing
  (Schiffman), 64
Success principles, 125–26
Suspects, 48

Team selling, 113–16
Telemarketing
  initial contacts, 54, 64–65, 89
  sales cycle, 74
Telus Mobility, 123
Time, for sales completion, 15, 87–89
Timetable, 71
20:5:1 ratio, 25
25 percent column, 81–84, 86

GETTING TO
"CLOSED"

Purchase for your entire sales force and watch sales soar! For quantities of *Getting to "Closed"* please contact Terri Joseph in Special Sales, 800-621-9621, ext. 4307, or tjoseph@dearborn.com.

You may also order this book with a customized cover featuring your company name, logo, and message.

Dearborn™
Trade Publishing
A **Kaplan Professional** Company